"If you've been searching for a clear explanation of the core message of Jesus, look no further. Here is a book of fascinating stories, some old, some new, that will take you to the heart of what Jesus called 'good news.' The search for spiritual peace is universal. Finding an end to inner restlessness is much less common. This is a helpful guide to experiencing the missing peace of life's puzzle."

—Marcus Brotherton, author of the award-winning *Feast for Thieves*

"One of the greatest needs in our world is for people in touch with the living God to share their faith. This book is going to be a great help to people all over the world who are willing to do that. Please not only read it but pass it on to someone else."

—George Verwer, founder of Operation Mobilisation

"It's not Jan's knack for stringing words together—though he's certainly good at it—that makes this book a treasure. It's his knack for pinning down exactly why so many Christians feel frustrated with a life that seemed to promise so much more. This book is going to help a lot of people."

—Mark Atteberry, award-winning author
of *The Samson Syndrome*

"In *Still Restless*, Jan Hettinga provides a compelling and eminently readable response to what some have called 'the insufficiency of all things attainable,' which has become the chief malaise of contemporary culture. With powerful, practical stories from his many years as a spiritual leader and teacher, he leads the reader on a gentle journey toward satiating the inner restlessness that stalks so many people today by inviting them to find rest in Jesus and his kingdom. Jan helps us identify the sources that spawn our spiritual restlessness and then deftly leads us on the journey to finding the source of satisfaction for this holy longing. I highly recommend this book to everyone who longs to be restless no more!"

—Dr. Sam Rima, lead pastor of North Seattle Alliance Church
and author of *Overcoming the Dark Side of Leadership*
and *Leading from the Inside Out*

"In life and in writing, Dr. Jan Hettinga is a gifted and humble man who loves Jesus and draws great wisdom from God's Word. In *Still Restless*, Jan beautifully melds powerful stories from Scripture with those of his own life in ministry. By example, Jan demonstrates how to give clear, thoughtful answers to complex life issues by relying on the wisdom found in the kingdom gospel of Scripture. This book is an inspiring guide for those who have attempted to play God in their own lives or at least have sought to slow his advances. For those of us in ministry, *Still Restless* holds up a mirror to our own motivations, while allowing us to become better prepared to respond to those who seek God or have yet failed to recognize that they need him. I strongly recommend this book to all who know Jesus as Lord, and to those who have yet to meet him. Yes, that means everyone."

—Gary Irby, director of Seattle Church Planting and
Northwest Baptist Church Planting

"The kingdom message is not just another gospel technique, it is the way Jesus chose to connect with those he met. Eleven men understood this message and changed the world. Our work here is not done! Imagine what the church would look like today if this message were shared in the pulpit and lived in the marketplace. As long as there are lost souls and broken hearts, may the church feel restless as well. Thank you, Jan, for being obedient."

—Lee Harris, Kingdom Builders Ministries

"*Still Restless* is written from a pastor's heart. Nestle in, and let Jan Hettinga unlock the Scriptures and take you to the God who is, who may be different from the God you've known."

—Laurie Short, author of *Finding Faith in the Dark*

MARLENE STEVE.
LOVE YOU AND
SEEKING HIS KINGDOM 1ST!
Jan
MATT. 6:33

STILL RESTLESS

Conversations That Open the Door to Peace

Jan David Hettinga

Kregel
Publications

For my children,
Nathan, Holly, and Jeremy,
who found their home in God's kingdom.

A lady I know . . . refused to talk about life beyond death with her children because, she said, she didn't want them to be disappointed if it turned out not to be there. Well now. . . . If there is no afterlife they certainly won't be disappointed. If there is, they may find themselves badly prepared. The only possible way they could be disappointed is if they do continue to exist.

If, indeed, what happens at physical death is the cessation of the person, then approaching death is, at worst, like going to the surgeon. It is unpleasant, but at least it will be over soon, and there will then be no pain, no suffering, no regrets. No you. No anything, so far as you are concerned.

The truly brave person is surely the one who can cheerfully face the prospect of an unending existence. Suppose you are never going to stop existing and there is nothing you can do about it—except possibly make your future existence as desirable an existence as possible? That would call for real courage.

—Dallas Willard, *The Divine Conspiracy*

CONTENTS

Foreword by Dr. Scott Ridout   *11*

Acknowledgments   *17*

Introduction   *Shopping for Spirituality*   *19*

Part One: Sources of Restlessness

1   Restless About God   *25*

2   Playing God   *35*

3   Walking Away from God   *43*

4   Arguing with God   *53*

5   Angry with God   *63*

6   Blaming God   *73*

7   Abusing God   *81*

8   At Odds with God   *91*

CONTENTS

Part Two: Coming to the End of Restlessness

9 Curious About God   *101*
10 Thirsty for God   *111*
11 Questioning God   *121*
12 Seeing God   *133*
13 Ready to Meet God   *143*
14 Giving Up to God   *153*
15 Respect for God   *163*
16 Coming to God   *173*

Epilogue   *The End of Restlessness*   *183*

Discussion Questions   *187*
A Fresh Start with God   *197*
About the Author   *199*

FOREWORD

When I was young I had a drug problem. My parents *drug* me to church every weekend. It made sense. After all, I was the son of a pastor who was trying his best to lead congregations into much needed personal, congregational, and community change, so church became a family endeavor. Every Sunday morning Mom would throw the four of us in the back of the Country Squire station wagon in our Sunday best (I am still in counseling for the plaid bow ties and suits), give us the "behave" lecture, and send us off to class.

My dad was great at his job. Everywhere we went, the churches he led grew. In fact, he got the reputation of being a great fundraiser and became the leader of choice any time a church needed an expansion campaign. He rose very quickly in the ranks of our denomination and, as a result, was in great demand all over the state. I was very proud of my dad. Yet somewhere in that journey of ministry success, I got lost. I can't say that it was my dad's fault—I don't think it was. But the result of that season was unsettledness in my experience with church. You could even say I was cynical about church, but still curious about God. I was restless.

We all have unique experiences with God and church, but mine felt, well, personal. Outside our home my father's public persona was one of great confidence and compelling will; at home I saw and experienced the wear and tear of ministry on my family. I would listen through the walls as my mom and dad would wrestle with the issues of church. High expectations, constant meetings (they were called *committees* back then), and difficult personalities had a growing negative effect on my family and ultimately on my faith.

By the time I graduated from high school, I made the decision to go a different direction. I was done with church. I had played the game long enough. I wanted more from life than a perfunctory routine. After eighteen years of observation and participation I decided that feeling close to God wasn't worth the cost of having to look like I had it all together—even if it was only for an hour on Sunday. I had an opinion about church: it didn't work. I even came up with a term for my experience; in conversation I would say that I was "church-damaged." I wanted a better life and my sense was that my church experience didn't contribute to that goal. So when I left for college, with all the wisdom and experience of an eighteen-year-old, I left church.

But God wasn't done with me.

It was during my freshman year at Virginia Tech that I met John Heyward. John was also a civil engineering student at VT who was a couple years ahead of me in the program, but light-years ahead of me in faith. John had discovered Christ at this very secular university (which sounds unlikely, but it happens all the time!). His faith was real and rich. His life, attitudes, values, beliefs, and behaviors were completely transformed by his newfound faith— so much so that he couldn't keep it to himself. In his enthusiasm, he formulated a plan to reach the entire campus with his message. He made the decision to call all 23,000 students on campus and ask if they would like to know Jesus personally! You would think that this random phone call strategy would have very little possibility of success. But then again, you weren't the first person he called . . . I was.

The phone rang on a bitter cold day in early January of my freshman year. I remember the exchange like it was yesterday. "My name is John and I have a four-point outline of the New Testament. Would you like to go through it?"

As I listened to those words, the pains of past church involvement flashed through my mind. I had gone to school to get away from religion. I was done with church and church people. My decision was settled and I had moved on to other more promising pursuits—girls, friends, fraternity life, and a degree that would ensure my ability to afford a fun-and-games lifestyle. Church had no place in my plan. My response was short and clear. "Nope," I replied.

To my surprise, this answer was not enough to shut down John's determination. My parents had always taken the sales calls at our home, so I did not know that I was supposed to hang up and move on with my life. This gave John time to throw in three words that would change the course of my life.

"Well, why not?" he asked.

Honestly I had never given that much thought. No one had ever challenged me to get below the surface of my church experience. I don't ever recall a conversation about faith outside the Sunday school room (which later I would discover is the norm for many church people). This conversation was outside my religious routine and I found myself in unfamiliar territory. So I gave the only answer I could find. "Well, I'm a pastor's kid and I probably know it already." *That should be enough to shut him down*, I thought.

"Really? That's great! I am new at this Christian thing and I have lots of questions. Can I come over and talk to you about it?" John replied.

Talk about our faith? Who does that? Yet the excitement in his voice at this point shocked me and somehow I found myself agreeing to meet with this guy I didn't know to talk on a subject that I no longer had any interest in.

That conversation with John changed the course of my life. In the twenty minutes we had together I discovered something about myself. I discovered that although I had church experience, I had no experience with God. I had been in church all my life, but I had not met God. I didn't know Jesus, just some random facts about him. Church was a routine, a ritual, mere religion. John talked about Jesus as if he was in a relationship. I had no idea what he was talking about or how to relate to his experience. Yet when he left my room, my heart was stirred to think, *what if there is something more to this Jesus thing?*

Over the next several months I met with John on a regular basis. His faith was vibrant and his passion for God was real. It seemed like almost daily he would walk into my dorm room, Bible in hand, and say, "Look what I found in God's Word!" His enthusiasm was contagious and I found myself opening my Bible (the one I got at confirmation when I was eight but never opened—yeah, it had been packed in with my college things—thanks, Mom). For the first time in my life, I began reading it for myself. I was restless, but now in a good way.

It wasn't long before I realized my need for a savior. As a nineteen-year-old, I acknowledged Jesus as the one who died for my sin. More importantly, I committed to trust his wisdom and leadership in every area of my life. That second decision proved crucial for me. I didn't want the level of faith I had seen all my life in church; I wanted a vibrant, life-changing, personal experience that would transform me and bring out the best of God's design in me. I went beyond making a decision to believe; I became a committed follower of Jesus Christ.

Thirty-two years later, I am still on that journey and my passion for the Christ-led life continues to grow. I look back and see the restlessness of my soul in those early years and the frustration of being religious but not pursuing a relationship with God. I am dumbfounded as to how I almost missed the point of church. Jesus didn't want to just get me into heaven after my life was over. Instead he wanted to get heaven into me while I live. God wants all of us to experience a fullness in life that only comes from him. And to my surprise, God's chosen instrument for moving us from making decisions to being disciples is . . . the church. My early church experience taught me that proximity doesn't promise maturity. Geography doesn't guarantee growth. I had to make an intentional effort to move forward in my faith.

What about you?

For those of you who are exploring Jesus for the first time, you will realize that God is not mad at you . . . he is mad about you! For those of you stuck in a spiritual funk, I hope this reading will refresh your faith. For those who approach life from the intellectual side, allow the words of this book to challenge your thinking and give you fresh perspective. If you, like me, would label yourself "church-damaged" by past experience, I pray that this book will erase the cynicism and mend the broken pieces of your soul.

Regardless of your experience, Jan Hettinga has a delightful way of challenging our status quo and getting us moving toward the healthy restlessness that God wants all of us to experience in life. Why should we settle for survival when God wants to do a significant work in and through our lives? The decision that many of us made to acknowledge Christ as Savior is not a finish line but the starting gate to the greatest race a human being can ever be a part of. Yet to experience all that Christ has for us will take more than our intention. It will require our attention.

I pray that this book will help you break down the barriers that are preventing you from experiencing the fullness of life that God desires for you.

Scott Ridout
President, Converge

ACKNOWLEDGMENTS

At first a book is an idea, a brainchild of the imagination. Then it becomes a discussion with trusted friends. And finally it is hard work.

My wife, Scharme, would not let me give up on this book. She resurrected it after each death and burial.

My friend and literary agent, Greg Johnson of WordServe Literary Group, Ltd., has always believed in my life message. He is a classic encourager.

Marcus Brotherton worked with me to get a professional proposal put together. Teaming up with him was a dream come true.

Judith Couchman agreed to the tough labor of editing the manuscript. It was like having private writing lessons. Her experience and skill made this a far better book.

My gratitude extends to these and others who read the work and made helpful suggestions.

INTRODUCTION

SHOPPING FOR SPIRITUALITY

My wife and I were "in the market" for a car, after saving up for years. We drove from dealer to dealer, examining and test-driving at least a dozen different cars. It wasn't long before we got seriously confused with TMI (too much information). We needed help.

What started out as an adventure morphed into frustration. We faced an unexpectedly steep learning curve, and we didn't have time to drive and compare so many makes and models.

We favored one, but after trying another we realized its advantages and strong points too. After several changes of mind, we needed to find and trust an expert on late model vehicles. But who? This wasn't my usual approach to shopping.

When I shop for an item I expect to encounter biases. A salesperson represents a store's product line, trained to present its brands as superior to the competition. I listen to the pitch, watch the demonstration, and then sometimes go online to examine the options before making a decision. That is, if time permits. After examining at least a few available choices, I make a partially informed decision and hope I'm happy with it.

Because you're reading this book—or at least flipping through its pages—you're probably searching for an adequate spirituality. Your quest for a functioning, satisfying inner life may take you to books, assorted websites, and brand-name religious groups. As if on a spiritual shopping trip, you're checking out the options. And like those store sales personnel, I'm confident this guidebook contains the essentials for one option: the teachings of Jesus Christ, the founder of Christianity.

I feel confident because I accept these teachings as the foundation of an effective lifestyle for myself. Through the years I've researched and integrated these truths into my life, and helped others follow Christ too. Now I'm presenting his teachings in book form, to help you make a solid choice as you evaluate Christianity. At the same time, this is not a comprehensive study of all Christian teachings and principles. Rather, it focuses on Jesus Christ and his actual message, recorded in source materials that evolved into the Bible. And it offers an end to the disquiet and angst of a restless longing for something . . . more.

The offer was there in Jesus's day, and it's still there today. To shed light on the biblical teachings as they relate to contemporary life, I have chosen to use stories of people I have met. In order to do that and respect their privacy, I have rearranged details of their identity. Sometimes I changed their gender, their age, or their life situation. Sometimes I morphed two or even three similar stories together. Their identities are protected, but, be assured, these conversations with their emotions and personal reactions and responses did take place in real lives. Their stories demonstrate that all of us have issues when it comes to God. We can identify with each other's journeys and learn from one another's choices and resulting outcomes.

As you read, you'll encounter my biases and presuppositions. I am a Christian. I want to explain the Bible, and especially Christ's teachings, as the best answer to life's biggest questions: Does my life hold meaning and purpose? What's gone wrong with our world? Is there a God? If so, of all the ones available in the religious marketplace, which one is he? Is it possible to know the true God and to relate to him? If God exists, what does he expect of me? Can he resolve my problem of restlessness?

When you cut through more than twenty centuries of religious language grown up around and sometimes cluttering Christianity, you'll find a cluster of sound, core ideas. And remarkably, a simple belief system. I encourage you to check the Bible references as you read, to discover what this sourcebook really says. Then, like a well-informed shopper, you can choose for yourself—based on what Christ really claims rather than what other people think or tell you to believe.

Jesus presents clear instruction about accessing a satisfying personal faith. He calls it the *gospel*—the good news—of the kingdom. He points to a door to peace for life now and forever, but few choose to enter it (Matt. 7:13–14). After reading this book, you'll understand why some people turn away and others step forward—and you can make your choice. The deep restlessness of the soul can be left behind and inner peace can come to stay.

PART ONE

SOURCES OF RESTLESSNESS

There is no meaning in anything if the universe has not a centre of significance and an authority that is the author of our rights.
— G. K. Chesterton, *What I Saw in America*

Nothing upsets us more than to be told . . . that "our purposes differ from those of the Almighty."
— Abraham Lincoln, quoted in Walter B. Wriston, *Risk & Other Four-Letter Words*

There are only two kinds of people in the end: those who say to God, "Thy will be done," and those to whom God says, in the end, "Thy will be done."
— C. S. Lewis, *The Great Divorce*

ONE

RESTLESS ABOUT GOD

I don't need to close my eyes to remember.

So many names, faces, conversations—people I met in forty-plus years of pastoral ministry. People who sat in my office, or talked to me in the lobby after a morning service, or phoned me at home to pour out restless hearts. Saint Augustine, the fourth-century theologian and philosopher said it well: "Our hearts are restless, O Lord, until they find rest in Thee."[1]

Early in my office one evening a young university professor visited me. Not yet thirty, Allan held a string of degrees and had traveled the fast track to a position at the University of Washington. He and his wife had recently married and both qualified as young intellectual giants. Their future looked bright, except for one problem.

Restlessness.

---

1. Augustine, *Confessions,* edited and translated by Philip Burton (New York: Alfred A. Knopf, 2001), book I, chapter 1.

"We've been attending your church lately, but I'm not sure exactly why," Allan said. "I guess you could say we've been searching for something beyond ourselves, but we don't know what that is, or even how to articulate what we're looking for. We just know there's got to be something beyond what we have now."

I responded, "It sounds like you're looking for God. You want to discover God for yourselves, is that it?"

"Maybe," he said. "But I doubt if he can be known. If God exists, then he must be beyond size, intelligence, or goodness. Surely it's beyond the capacity of human minds to understand him."

Many people have the same kinds of doubts.

People like Clarice and Brandon, parents of young children. I met this couple at their house for coffee after they tucked the children into bed. Brandon worked at a secure job as an engineer at Boeing. Clarice lived her dream as a stay-at-home mom. Busy and tired, they keenly focused on organizing their lives around soccer and suburban living, their work and house, trips to the grocery store and vacations to visit grandparents. They lived the American dream. However, they couldn't enjoy life for fear it would fall apart. They worried the good life might not last.

"I'm so anxious all the time," Clarice said. "It's like we're working so hard to build this kingdom of home and family. But I'm always worried the other shoe is going to drop. Like something bad is going to happen. I just know it. If God is out there, does he really interact with us? Does he really care?"

Did you catch the word *kingdom*? File that word away for later.

I remember Katie, an intelligent and capable young woman who couldn't fathom why a good God could allow so much suffering in the world. She wanted results. She insisted on a God who ended tragedy and suffering on a global scale. Until then, Katie would try everything she could to hasten this along. Still, she couldn't understand why God didn't intervene sooner and more often.

I talked with Connor, just released from a halfway house. Connor believed he'd done too much wrong in his life for God to accept him. A rebel to the core, Connor assured me he "had no problem with God," but God probably "had a problem" with him. "Is there a way out of the hole I've dug?" he asked.

I spoke with Lucas after he landed in the hospital. A gifted young football player, his life and identity revolved around sports. He possessed the size, skill, and speed to join the NFL, but a spinal cord injury shattered that dream. "I don't know who I am anymore," he said. "I don't know what to do or where to go or what's important in life anymore. Why would God ever allow this to happen to me?"

I listened to Gabe, a middle-aged man who had attended church since birth. He knew everything about religious life, but still felt far away from God. "Surely the church should show me the answer," he said. "Why would the church fail to help me figure out what's missing in my life?"

I felt compassion for Natalie, divorced twice by age thirty-three and desperate to marry again. Natalie thought if she found the right husband life would fall into place. If God cared, then surely he would answer her prayer. Wouldn't he?

So much restlessness. So many people searching for something beyond themselves, something to improve life or make more sense of it. But they couldn't identify this "something," or how to gain it if they recognized it.

People build kingdoms that crumble.

The problem of restlessness can be summarized like this: every person seeks security, significance, and purpose. Each of us craves a happy, meaningful life. So we construct a kingdom. Everybody builds a kingdom. Everybody.

Think of a kingdom as a way of organizing life, a system to make sense of the world. It's a way of living we set up and run ourselves. In a personal kingdom we take control, and we like it that way, thanks.

We articulate a kingdom in these ways, and more:

- When I earn enough money, I'll feel truly secure.
- If I marry the right person and we build a home together, I'll be happy.
- Because I'm smart, and surround myself with brilliant people, I'm significant.
- My family's prominence in society makes me influential and respected.
- A great career and growing reputation mark me as somebody important.
- Winning at whatever I set out to accomplish proves I'm successful.

A kingdom rises up when we hold something tightly in our hands. It could be our ambition, athletic ability, car, career, children, education, home, spouse, or wealth—even a rank or reputation and the influence it garners.

Once we construct a kingdom, we cling to and defend it when attacked. Our kingdom works for a while because it delivers what we hoped for. But then our carefully constructed, controlled world eventually crumbles and falls apart. Our kingdom never lasts because it can't; it's built on earthly values that disintegrate.

Life changes, and so a kingdom transitions. Sometimes life changes simply because one season ends and we head into another. But other times life changes because of difficulty. Maybe a tragedy descends. Or an accident. Or an overwhelming pressure. Something that's too tough to handle. That's usually when a kingdom exposes its frailty.

That's also when we grow restless. Worried. Fearful. We grab and clutch things, hoping to hold on to a kingdom and keep it from collapsing. We wonder what else exists out there, and what we might do to get it. Sometimes we act out, attend counseling, or take drastic steps. Maybe we get divorced, hoping for relief from conflict, or turn to the bottle or porn or gaming or gambling or another numbing, addictive behavior. These behaviors are symptoms of a crumbling kingdom.

Life isn't working out the way we hoped it would.

I believe this restlessness that sometimes results in taking drastic measures can lead us to God, and eventually to Jesus, his Son.

I mention this solution up front because we vary in our opinions about Jesus—we seekers and skeptics and others who long to know the truth. Some settle well with Jesus, his identity and what he did. Others stay far away from him and like it that way.

Either direction, ultimately Jesus answers restlessness. We each hang on tightly to a "kingdom." We replace God with something, letting it eclipse his loving role in our hearts. But to truly make life work—to overturn this restlessness and find what we're longing for—we must exchange our kingdom for God's kingdom. We give our kingdom back to its rightful owner.

This isn't easy. It requires humility, an inner attitude that doesn't present itself naturally.

It requires change, what the Bible calls repentance.

Ouch. That's a hard word. Some would say an archaic word. Even a spiteful word. But it's a word God uses. It means I release my life to God and let him lead. I agree with him that my own personal kingdom doesn't work. I acknowledge he is God, not me. Or to use kingdom-oriented terminology, I step off the throne and let him be king.

The heart of Jesus's message travels the path to peace and God's kingdom. Jesus wants to give us our lives back, the lives we waste in attempts to set up kingdoms. His model prayer, the Lord's Prayer, simply and profoundly expresses this step of surrender: "Your kingdom come, your will be done, on earth as it is in heaven" (Matt. 6:10). The term *earth* includes us: our bodies, minds, and souls. God's will "done on earth" means my earth and your earth, not just the planet Earth. Therein lies the solution for the restless problems in human history and individual lives.

When God takes over, his kingdom arrives and his will cultivates a way of life. Instead of fighting against God's best for us, like rebellious teenagers, we give up and give in. We invite him to take charge in the heart's throne room. Everything functions according to his original design. Life focuses on a relationship with God rather than on conflict. His kingdom is the best possible residence for us.

A voice speaks to our restlessness.

Many people think of God only as "big." Throughout the centuries, theologians have called this incomprehensible bigness of God "immensity." For understandable reasons, God's immensity seems like an insurmountable barrier to people who seriously want to know him.

But Jesus changes this because we can approach him. Remember high school English class and Mark Twain's classic novel *The Prince and the Pauper*? The storyline about a king who leaves his palace and lives disguised among ordinary people captivates imaginations. In this famous novel, the Prince of Wales (Edward VI) disguises himself and dwells among the people of his kingdom. Mark Twain's tale offers the adventure of a lost heir to the throne, finally recognized and crowned.

That novel compares to Jesus's story. He's the King of everything who set majesty aside and deliberately became a man, God-in-the-flesh. He left the palace and throne of heaven so a human mother could deliver him as a defenseless, vulnerable baby. It's the story of God stepping away from his immensity, away from looking too big for us.

If we only think of God as a Supreme Being, it's easy to consider him unapproachable. But in Jesus's story, God intentionally turns accessible and available. God-in-Jesus likens to God next door to us. Jesus is God with skin on, God observable, God touchable, God down to earth. God knowable.

With this realization, life can take a good turn. Because when Jesus connects humanity to God, we hear the unthinkable.

We hear a voice.

This voice offers music to the soul, resonating deep within and calming restlessness. The voice talks about how God, according to Jesus, expresses more interest in us than we in him. Jesus invites us home to the realm he calls the kingdom of God.

The voice simply says, Talk to me.

It's good to know who wants to talk to us.

Today when we think of leaders, we often expect dominance, managed images, scripted charisma, and an aggressive willingness to win. But Jesus presents a welcome and refreshing change. Think about him for a moment.

In the thirty-three years Jesus lives in a human body, he accomplishes his mission. He reveals God's heart and communicates his message in an understandable size. As a human, Jesus removes the basis of our distrust. God's angels announce his arrival as a baby and then vanish. He lives like any other baby from a poor family: no privileges, silver spoons, royal advantages, displays of rank or wealth, or his heavenly Father's mega-influence.

Look at the facts of Jesus's life, recognized by both secular and Christian historians:

- Born in a stable. When Jesus's earthly father and pregnant mother travel to Bethlehem for a census count, they can't find lodging. Joseph and Mary finally settle into a rough-shod stable for the night, and she delivers Jesus among farm animals (Luke 2:1–20).

- Lives with a scandal about his birth. The New Testament book of Matthew refers to the public disgrace Joseph tries to avoid when Mary, his fiancée, turns up pregnant and he is not the father (Matt. 1:18–25).
- Grows up lower class, in a tradesman's family. Jesus's earthly father works as a carpenter and so does he (Matt. 13:55; Mark 6:3).
- Lives in a small, rural town. Joseph and Mary live in their hometown, Nazareth, in the region of Galilee. They raise Jesus there (Luke 2:39).
- Learns in synagogue schools. History informs us a boy in the Jewish culture receives his education in the local synagogue.
- Lives on handouts from generous people during his ministry, the last three years of his life. Apparently most of his financial support derives from devout women (Matt. 27:55; Luke 8:1–3).
- Hangs around with the poor, the disenfranchised, the sick, the mentally disturbed, and the notorious outcasts of society. In fact, religious leaders heavily criticize his choice of companions (Luke 5:29–30; 7:37–39).
- Endures relentless opposition from the power brokers in his culture. All four of the biographical books in the New Testament report the ruling-class enmity toward Jesus. A strong example exists in John 11, after Jesus raises Lazarus from the dead. The chapter ends with the religious leaders plotting to kill Jesus.
- Dies as a common criminal. Roman soldiers crucify Jesus between two thieves; this indicates that authorities consider him as guilty of capital crime as these criminals (Luke 23:32–33).
- Is buried in a borrowed tomb. Joseph of Arimathea lays the body of Jesus in his own new tomb (Matt. 27:57–60).

Clearly Jesus contrasts sharply with human arrogance, greed, and self-centeredness. Instead of using superior power and intelligence to force an agenda, Jesus lives humbly. He cares for people's needs, consistently acting more like a servant than a master.

It sounds paradoxical, but as a result of this humility, most people who meet Jesus never figure out his true identity. He startles and puzzles them. He doesn't act presidential. He doesn't position himself in the corridors of power. Nobody arranges press releases or photo ops. Literally, no one expects God, downsized to our level, to behave this way. The empowered people instinctively regard him as an irritation and a threat to their ambitions. He requires removal. So they dismiss, reject, and murder him.

The Bible summarizes it: "The Son is the radiance of God's glory and the exact representation of his being" (Heb. 1:3). That means the Creator God is humble, self-giving, and the safest kind of leader—because that's who Jesus is. If you see Jesus, then the Bible claims you are seeing God.

Is the kingdom we already have enough?

While Jesus walks the earth, he talks to many individuals. Each conversation takes on a different form, because everybody's kingdom-control issue is unique. At the same time, these God-to-human conversations act like mirrors. We see glimpses of ourselves in the interactions, and probably at least one of them closely fits our personal profile.

Think of Jesus as a living photo album displaying snapshots of God the Creator. As we look through the album and view God revealed through Jesus, we can't help but compare his image to ourselves. God's safe, loving, compassionate nature contrasts with ours. Instead of compiling reasons to fear God, we recognize our souls as capable of dark and even dangerous behavior, thoughts, and attitudes.

In not trusting Jesus, we project onto him the attitudes and motives of our hearts. Yet when Jesus shows us the inner qualities of God's heart, he shuts down our misplaced suspicion. We realize only our runaway self-absorption is dangerous.

When we compare our own kingdom in sharp contrast to the heavenly kingdom Jesus offers, we recognize the need to relinquish our restless control in exchange for the peace of his kingdom. What happens if we seriously ask God for his kingdom? That's the big invitation. We can pray for God's kingdom to come and his will to be done because his love, expressed in the sacrificial generosity of Jesus, makes it possible. Without Jesus, we remain shut out, stuck with our own crumbling kingdom instead of his.

Jesus offers his invaluable eternal kingdom in exchange for ours. But this presents a dilemma. We already hold a carefully constructed kingdom. We control a pile of stuff. To receive God's kingdom, he gently asks us to let go. We change our mind about who gets control and which kingdom to value and embrace. We open our hands and hold them up to Jesus like a grateful child receiving a good gift from a parent. We say, "God I want whatever you have for me. I trust your love. I know you have my best interest at heart. I want what you have planned and prepared for me."

That's true change, real repentance.

I personally discovered God looks for "non-compete" hearts. When I stopped trying to hold on to my kingdom and add his on top of mine, everything changed. At first I thought it would be smart to live both ways: keep mine and add on his kingdom. But he wouldn't play that game. I'm glad I accepted his invitation to forsake my control and rejoin the kingdom he created me to enjoy. I harbor no regrets about abandoning my kingdom and entering his by the choice he calls *faith*.

The Father in heaven loves open hands. When our self-sufficiency ends, we eagerly want his will to be done. This opens the floodgates of his generosity. God gives us far more than we could ever ask or think (Eph. 3:20).

God's kingdom answers our questions. He satisfies the heart. We live at peace. Our restlessness subsides.

TWO

PLAYING GOD

Body pierced, tattooed, hair impossibly red, Cassie looked like a poster child for the postmodern culture. An art student from Wales, she jostled alongside me in the back of an express bus in England. When Cassie discovered my occupation, she plied me with questions.

"Can you tell me if there are any shortcuts through the tangle of spiritualties out there?" she asked. "I mean, it seems like you have to trust somebody . . . but who really knows enough about God to help me cut through the bs?"

I looked at Cassie with a mixture of surprise and admiration. From her public persona, she seemed like the last person to seriously pursue the Creator.

"What would convince you that you've found the real thing?" I asked.

She tossed her flaming hair, looked hard into my eyes, and said, "I'd like to see a spirituality that shuts down evil and empowers good."

I almost asked a question, but she continued.

"What I mean is . . . it's gotta work. It's gotta change people . . . lots of people, so life is livable on this stinking planet again!" She breathed hard, exposing the depth of her passion. I realized she wanted the same thing I pursued: a good God unleashed; an unstoppable, world-changing final answer.

What will work to change the world?

More than ever, people hunger for an authentic connection with God. Yet the younger generations don't easily compartmentalize spiritual matters like their parents and grandparents. They want their own experience with spiritual reality. But they also expect faith to make a difference beyond religious activities. They want transformation in relationships, families, communities, and cultures.

It's shocking, really. After organized religion successfully tamed God, people still want power in their belief systems. As with all generations, they crave personal healings and private miracles, but that's not enough. They want cities healed and the world changed—impossibly changed! They feel burned out with political and bureaucratic promises of a better world that never arrives. They want something more potent than campaign promises or special interest lobbyists.

"What kind of changes would be big enough?" I asked Cassie.

"I'll have to think about that," she said. It was clear she was not ready to deal with a plan or process for significant, world-wide change.

After a while she said, "If we could eliminate poverty and social injustice and clean up the environment before the oceans die, I think it would be a good start." Cassie noticed I waited for more and she looked faintly embarrassed.

Eventually she commented, "I don't want to sound like a radical college student, and I don't know how to put words to it. But something big needs to happen. I feel it in my gut. I don't want to let the world just go to hell like it's doing now!"

Since that conversation, I've thought long and hard about what would change the world enough. I concluded it begins with the heart.

We each desire control.

At the core of every human resides a control center, the place where a person makes choices. The Bible calls this inner space the *heart*. It also says God wants a relationship with us from the inside out. Change initiating from the heart ultimately affects our actions. Just as on-board computers control the engines of high-tech automobiles, regulating the best combination of fuel, air, and spark, God desires to guide us at the heart level. Unfortunately, humans deliberately modified the original design. Long ago we unplugged ourselves and took over inner control. This explains the tragedy of our disturbing history. Although we fail to successfully occupy God's throne, we keep trying. We ruthlessly guard control of our hearts.

Think about it. We built the wonders of Egypt, the splendors of Greece, and the glories of Rome. We erected the magnificence of China, the marvels of India, and the monuments of the Incas and Aztecs. We designed and manufactured trains, planes, and automobiles. Our spaceships flew to the moon and back. But every empire in every age spreads a legacy of conflict, injustice, slavery, tyranny, oppression, and exploitation.

Without God's supervision, people inevitably attempt to control one another. No matter what system prevails—communism, socialism, monarchy, fascism, dictatorship, or democracy—people get hurt. Solutions to the world's problems seem as bad as, or worse than, the problems themselves.

When we reject the benevolent governance of the Creator, we

easily slip into arrogantly "playing God" with lives, including our own. Ironically, in the end we still end up governed, regulated, and restricted by others—the boundaries we struggled to avoid. In spite of history's pain, we still control each other primarily through government, and often overbearingly. For example, your choices and my decisions can collide. Because I don't trust you with the freedom of choice I insist on exercising myself, your independence threatens mine. So my people feel justified in controlling the behavior of your people. Here lie the seeds of oppressive government.

If you try dominating me to get what you want, I resent it. I fight back. It feels like the only self-respecting response. I want to break free from your attempts to restrict me, especially if you're abusive and intolerable. How dare you! What right do you have to control me? I should control you. In fact, I will restrict you to ensure my freedom.

So the conflict and pain continue. Parents and children arguing, husbands and wives sparring, neighbors battling, genders fighting, races rivaling, and nations warring.

When we look carefully at the historical perspective, we can trace painful and shameful behavior to a desire for unrestricted personal freedom. In a threatened moment it seems like a sacred right. In fact, it seems necessary. We rationalize and excuse our controlling behavior as we condemn and prosecute others for the same violations.

In contrast, what if we accepted God as our highest authority? After all, he designed and placed us on earth (Gen. 1–2). The Bible says he knows the number of hairs on our heads (Luke 12:7) and the number of our days (Ps. 139:16). Most of all, he pursues us with an unrelenting, unfathomable love (1 John 4:9–19). Given God's love and intimate attention to us—and our heartbreaking track record in recorded history—why not try what the Bible names as the original plan for human behavior? Why not accept God's way? So far we've succeeded in making one another miserable.

Perhaps God can show us a better way to live.

If this description of human behavior rings true to you—if you sense it's mostly accurate about the core of our universal dysfunctions—then you might be ready for Jesus. He speaks on behalf of God the Father (John 8:28–29). Jesus diagnoses the cause of our pain and despair as a kingdom problem. From God's perspective, we declared our independence from him and established our own reign.

Those mentored by Jesus recorded essential elements of his message. Stories about Jesus fill the beginning of the New Testament, the second half of the Bible. The books Matthew, Mark, Luke, and John—known as the Gospels—paint a portrait of him. Each book summarizes the life story and public message of Jesus in a unique way. His message to humanity remains remarkably consistent. Even if you read casually, Jesus's kingdom vocabulary stands out. For example:

- "'The time has come,' he said. 'The kingdom of God has come near. Repent and believe the good news'" (Mark 1:15).
- "Repent, for the kingdom of heaven has come near" (Matt. 4:17).
- "Very truly I tell you, no one can see the kingdom of God unless they are born again" (John 3:3).
- "After this, Jesus traveled about from one town and village to another, proclaiming the good news of the kingdom of God" (Luke 8:1).

The Bible records dozens of similar statements about Jesus's message. But what did this kingdom theme mean, and how does it apply to us?

When Jesus announces the kingdom of God is near, he refers to his arrival on earth. Combined with other statements, he actually claims to be King of the universe (John 18:36–37), and this presents an all-important choice.

When he uses the word *repent* it's as if he says, "You can run your life as you see fit, or you can change your mind and let me lead." That sounds like an ultimatum, doesn't it? He certainly makes no effort to avoid confrontation.

Humans wrestle with control issues at the heart level. Jesus knows his message feels threatening. Still, he doesn't hesitate to state boldly and without apology that God wants to establish his kingdom in the heart of every person. With this change, resistance, revolution, and independence could end within his listeners—and us. A new era of God's reign could begin. This is the door to peace, the entrance to God's kingdom. Jesus swings the door wide open with a personal invitation: "Come to me, all of you who are weary and carry heavy burdens, and I will give you rest. Take my yoke upon you. Let me teach you, because I am humble and gentle at heart, and you will find rest for your souls" (Matt. 11:28–29 NLT).

There it is: the promise of inner peace that ends our restlessness. It is exactly what those who come to Jesus in faith discover for themselves. But there is a problem. There's a kingdom to let go of in order to receive his kingdom.

Framing the issue with this kingdom language touches the nerve of human rebellion.

According to the record, Jesus intentionally focuses his message on God's view of the earth's problems, and what can solve them. He chooses the word *repentance* as the most appropriate response. Technically, *repent* means to change your mind or direction, or in this case, to change sides.

If we buy into Jesus's message, then changing sides results from clear-eyed sanity. From the inner control center, a heart response sounds like this: "God, you should be my leader. I'm sorry I've tried to take your place."

The Bible calls sin "going our own way" and breaking with God's leadership. In today's culture we view sin as a judgmental concept. We tend to consider our mistakes and violations as justifiable. Yet we're willing to call other people's bad behavior a crime and offense, especially if it negatively impacts us. Could it be that living out from under God is the deepest source of our sense of malaise, our feelings that something important is missing? Could this be the cause of our restlessness?

According to Jesus, repentance involves more than feeling sorry about what we've done or not done. If we only express regret—even with tears—without a change of behavior, we do not truly repent. Regret usually accompanies true repentance, but from Jesus's perspective repentance marks the arrival of God's kingdom and his leadership. So Jesus asks a crucial question: "Will you give up your inner bent toward control? Will you permit me to lead you? I offer a better way."

There's an ultimate memory chip in our DNA.

I find Jesus's message worth trusting because it cracks open a solution large enough for our biggest problems.

Jesus insists God's kingdom always existed, exists now, and will always exist. God's government forms the bedrock of existence, consciousness, meaning, and purpose. If this proves true, then laws governing our bodies and the environment flow from God's kingdom laws. Our cells, glands, organs, nerves, and vital systems function according to the King's specifications. Our minds, wills, and emotions operate by principles he designed.

I suspect we know this genetically. Somehow, this awareness lingers in our DNA, a longing for something best understood as home. In our culture, people try to find inner peace and belonging through music, nature, sexuality, drugs, community service, supporting a good cause, or anything promising connection. People look desperately for things to make them happy, often without realizing what they're missing spiritually.

In contrast, Jesus connects inner peace with re-entry to heaven's realm. He talks as if his listeners already know about the kingdom. He launches the public explanation of his message, knowing this good news will connect to a needy place: the soul's homesickness for its lost spiritual birthplace. This presentation of heaven as our real home explains the need to build kingdoms. Like the industrious beaver, we were wired by the Creator to build things. We cut and shape our environments to reconstruct the concept of heaven buried in our subconscious. Without spiritual intervention, we set up inadequate kingdoms, avoiding the true kingdom where we can thrive.

Despite our misdirection, Jesus promises we can begin again. We can realize the design and purposes God planned for humanity. We can recover the original, joyous destiny Jesus invites us to find through the door to peace. We can abandon our failed experiments with independence and self-rule. He offers to replace them with "unexplainable peace" and a dependable antidote for fear and restlessness. He explains, "Peace I leave with you; my peace I give you. I do not give to you as the world gives. Do not let your hearts be troubled and do not be afraid" (John 14:27). One of his apprentices describes the offer this way: "And the peace of God, which transcends all understanding, will guard you hearts and your minds in Christ Jesus" (Phil. 4:7).

Jesus's followers call his offer the *gospel*. It means "good news"!

THREE

WALKING AWAY FROM GOD

If we could travel back in time and meet Jesus in the flesh, what would God-in-a-human-body say to us? If we asked him how to close the distance between us and the Creator, how would that conversation play out?

Without a doubt, he would respond to an interest in God and the afterlife, much like he approached people of his day. The record of his life reveals he took time for honest seekers. But to the degree that a person insisted on a personal agenda, Jesus altered the manner of his response. Learning how Jesus replied to varied seekers helps to identify tightly held priorities and control issues that resist his message. Here's where we will find a profile that matches our own. For example, meet the rich young ruler from Mark 10:17–31.

Finding eternal wealth is not easy.

The rich young ruler seems to have it all. He sits at the top of the heap, possessing all the money he can spend, plus all the power, prestige, and privilege society can grant him. Yet he searches for something more.

Consequently, when the rich man runs to Jesus, he falls to his knees and asks, "Good teacher, what must I do to inherit eternal life?"

I wonder why a person with impressive credentials would drop to his knees for anyone. Something must seriously disturb his self-sufficient, carefully constructed world. My guess: a brush with death. Or perhaps he encounters Jesus while returning from the funeral of a friend or relative. Whatever the case, the afterlife occupies his thoughts.

The man's question explains his soul's urgency: "What must I do to get eternal life?" The rich young ruler thinks he has the world by the tail, but already the inevitability of death looms before him.

Jesus responds by checking what the questioner believes about his identity. Jesus replies, "No one is good—except God alone." In other words, "Did you call me teacher because you think I am God?" We dare not pass lightly over the issue of Jesus's identity. If he is just another man, even with an outstanding intellect and talent, his guess won't be any better than ours. On the other hand, if Jesus is God in human skin, his opinion carries inescapable authority.

Next Jesus reminds the young man of the Ten Commandments, checking his ethics, morality, and character. He lists the six commands that specify how humans should treat one another. He asks if the ruler lives by this pattern:

1. Do not murder.
2. Do not commit adultery.
3. Do not steal.
4. Do not lie.
5. Do not defraud.
6. Honor your father and mother.

Apparently the young man knows the rudiments of his Jewish religion. With a straight face and a clear conscience, he claims keeping all six since boyhood. Jesus does not challenge the young ruler's track record or embarrass him by mentioning past failures. Instead, Jesus looks at him and loves him. He respects this sincere, diligent man for trying. Then Jesus pinpoints the issue preventing the young man from inheriting eternal life. "One thing you lack," Jesus says. "Go, sell everything you have and give to the poor, and you will have treasure in heaven. Then come, follow me."

We go back to the "big ten."

Does Jesus intend to start a religious order built on vows of poverty? Does he mean true goodness requires social justice and the redistribution of wealth? I'm convinced he does not refer to money and possessions. He focuses on kingdoms. Jesus knows that the rich man's significance and security depends on wealth's control and power. He essentially asks this man to give up his personal power base, the source of his security and significance.

Jesus does not forget the four other commandments. With strong and radical advice, he insists this self-sufficient man follow no other gods but the real God (Exod. 20:3). The answer to the man's question rests not on his connection with others but in his relationship with God.

The ruler's personal kingdom wedges itself between his heart and the Creator. Jesus insists that God does not want a religious compartment in our kingdom. He settles for nothing less than oversight of everything, starting with giving him the keys to whatever castles our independent selves build.

Many think the Ten Commandments tell us how to live. In one

sense, they do. But God never intended them as a do-it-yourself ladder of good works. Instead, the Bible says God wisely designed the commands as a reliable means of flushing out a chronic obsession with living to please ourselves. These commandments reveal our resistance to God's control, like they did for the rich young ruler. But they also lead people to the freedom and peace of faith in Christ (Gal. 3:22–25).

The story ends with the young ruler's disappointment. Jesus quotes a higher price for the gift of eternal life than the man feels willing to pay. When he hears this, the man's face falls. He goes away sad, because he has great wealth.

The illustration of the two kingdoms and the door from one to the other appears throughout this book. Each conversation summarizes a different kind of personal kingdom. Jesus approached each individual differently because their interior kingdoms were not shaped the same. Neither are ours. Somewhere in this book you will likely find a kingdom profile that comes close to matching your own. It's my conviction that each of these stories is recorded in the Bible so that all of us can get a better grasp of what we are hanging on to and what we need to let go of when we come to the kingdom Jesus offers.

Can you see the size and strength of the rich young ruler's kingdom? It is a tough one to abandon in exchange for what Jesus offers. The followers of Jesus are as puzzled as the ruler is dismayed.

Now the punch line. Jesus turns to his apprentices and says, "How hard it is for the rich to enter the kingdom of God!" This amazes the disciples. But Jesus repeats, "Children, how hard it is to enter the kingdom of God! It is easier for a camel to go through the eye of a needle than for someone who is rich to enter the kingdom of God."

The followers of Jesus respond strongly, saying to one another, "Who then can be saved?" Good question. The answer lies in the nature of what's gone wrong between humanity and God.

The Rich Young Ruler
Mark 10:17–27

Kingdom of Self
• Wealth
• Possessions
• Prominence
• Power

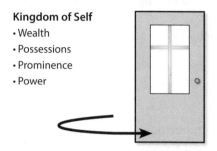

Kingdom of God
"You will have treasure in heaven."

• "What must I do to inherit eternal life?"
• Sell what you have, give it to the poor
• "Come, follow me."

If Jesus speaks the truth, we can't take our kingdom with us into God's kingdom, nor can we just add God's kingdom to ours. A little honesty exposes how we like making deals with God. We bargain, "I'll do this, this, and this for you, if you do such-and-such for me." In fact, we can turn faith into attempts to cut deals or harness God with our agendas, ambitions, and priorities. Our religious creativity amounts to keeping our kingdom and still trying to participate in God's kingdom at the end.

We think happiness relies on control of our kingdoms.

Jesus is right. It is hard—terribly hard—for us to relinquish what we so painstakingly piece together. We struggle to release our "wealth" to God in exchange for his promise of an eternal kingdom, especially if we think something less will do.

Even more, we build "wealth walls" around our inner castles. In the kingdom of self-in-control, we don't all construct the same walls. For example, we can build walls around these:

1. Education and intelligence
2. A successful career
3. Physical beauty
4. Creative giftedness
5. Athletic excellence
6. Family name and prominence
7. Religious tradition and service

Strangely enough, even pain and poverty can build unique inner castles, designed to protect us from the world. Individuals who control little in comparison to others can obsess over keeping what they own as fiercely as those with much to lose. Self-made kingdoms, whether desirable or undesirable, can grip us powerfully.

So, here is where that important Bible word *faith* figures in. Will I believe that behind the universe a good God keeps my best interests in mind? Will I trust him with control of my life? That takes real faith, doesn't it? According to Jesus, it's the only faith that matters.

Faith, the conviction we can trust God, makes it possible to relinquish our reign. When we repent, we change our mind about control. We give God permission to "be God" over us. With the control issue settled, we freely cooperate with our Eternal Leader. Our life fills with potential for huge significance in a dimension where death cannot rob us. We can fully embrace God's rule in this life, knowing it will seamlessly flow into the promised wonders of our next life.

If we surrender power, wealth, and whatever else provides temporary satisfaction, Jesus offers a door of faith into God's kingdom. The Bible declares that God's love allowed Jesus to be killed by Roman crucifixion (John 3:16). The Son of God deliberately used his victimization to purchase armistice for our sin. Jesus voluntarily took on the judgment we incurred by going our independent ways. The cross builds a way to return from the kingdoms of our own making to the kingdom of God. When we repent, we agree to be reconciled to God through Jesus's death on the cross and raised to a new kingdom life with him in the power of his resurrection.

Few of us would enter this door without assurance of a better option on the other side. If we release control, we want to know our new leader is good, trustworthy, and generous. God allowing his Son to die a painful death so we could enter his kingdom reveals the nature of his leadership. He is not self-centered; he is self-giving. Millions of Christians personally experience the love and leadership of a good God as the best way to live.

Meet Chris, a modern version of the rich young ruler.

As the only son of a state senator, Chris was groomed for a major role in national politics. After college, he won a seat in a state House of Representatives before he turned thirty. He reveled in government leadership; Chris loves the games of power and influence.

In everything, Chris keeps politics in mind. He chose his military service, wife, attorney credentials, and friends to enhance his political career. Politicians consider him an up-and-comer with a big future. With the help of a political marketing agency, he's building a national name for himself.

I met Chris while he was drumming up grassroots support for his campaign for governor. He visited my home as part of his door-to-door strategy. During our conversation he learned that we held similar political persuasions and that I led an influential church within his jurisdiction. Chris suggested we meet for lunch.

That meal lasted three hours. Chris told me he belonged to a prominent Christian church and believed in God and the Bible.

I sensed he considered church involvement a valuable political asset, a means of creating a solid-citizen image.

Chris then asked the question the rich young ruler presented to Jesus. He leaned back in his chair and inquired, "So, how can a person be sure he's going to heaven?" Even though he acted nonchalant, I sensed he would be disappointed if I didn't answer seriously.

I introduced Chris to the rich young ruler. He put down his fork and listened. By the time I finished, his eyes looked troubled. Clearly, Chris was counting the cost of entering God's kingdom. The Master was asking him for his personal kingdom. As a leader, Chris understood control issues. He recognized the logic of God's right to govern his own universe, including every human heart, even Chris's heart. Yet he felt stuck. How could he dare release his personal agenda to the supervision of Jesus?

He leaned forward and said, "Okay, Jan, I understand what you're saying. But this is way too much for Jesus to ask of me right now. Maybe later when I've achieved some of my life goals, I'll consider this again."

"Chris," I warned, "don't kid yourself. The bigger you build your kingdom, the harder it will be to let go of control. If you can't trust God with your future now and allow him to be more than window dressing in your life, I can almost promise you will be less likely to do so as time goes by."

Chris shook his head. "But what if God asked me to pursue something besides politics? If I really gave him control, he could have a completely different plan for me. I can't risk that. Not now. My career is too important to me."

It's worse than we think.

I can't say Chris left sad. Unfortunately, Chris thought so much of himself and his plans, he didn't seem worried about disappointing God. He may even have felt relieved.

I left the restaurant and drove home deep in thought. Once again I'd sat face-to-face with the core human problem. In fact, the longer I wrestle with my own issues, the more I'm convinced our obsession with control is far worse than we think.

Jesus is right: we hold on to our self-absorbed kingdom of the heart. As we struggle to submit it to the true leader, we feel a huge loss looming over our inner horizon, much like a death. But once we hand over our little kingdom to God, the value gained surpasses our dreams. When we release everything we control, we receive everything our new King controls. Jesus insists, "Your Father has been pleased to give you the kingdom" (Luke 12:32). What a magnificent offer! What a priceless exchange!

I'm not claiming everything will suddenly be wonderful when Jesus takes the driver's seat. Honestly, we acquire a new set of challenges when we follow Christ because many oppose him. The difference lies in the companionship we enjoy with God. He becomes a new source of strength, a wise guide and trustworthy companion. He promises, "Never will I leave you; never will I forsake you" (Heb. 13:5). We're no longer alone or restless. The loneliness of a castle-of-one vanishes in the companionship of a personal King.

Knowing this, we reach the door to peace and a crucial choice. Will we lean in and digest these concepts because they ring true? Or do we walk away, trying a more convenient and comfortable brand of spirituality?

FOUR

ARGUING WITH GOD

A certain temple lawyer has impressive credentials. He jumped through the required hoops to his destination. Top of his class. Brilliant scholar. A recognized expert in Jewish law. Knows the Old Testament like the back of his hand.

Now he hears about an upstart Galilean rabbi named Jesus, causing Jewish authorities terrible headaches. Other religious teachers and leaders attempt to humiliate Jesus to no avail. Now it's his turn. If he succeeds in discrediting Jesus, the top country leaders will thank him. He's waited for a break like this.

The man thinks intensively about Jesus: how to get at him, how to trip up and discredit this rabbi he considers a fake. After watching and listening to Jesus for a few weeks, he decides to act like a seeker, posing the same question he hears others ask. Then he can tear this impostor apart with his knowledge of the Law.

The moment arrives. During a lull in the buzz of conversation, Jesus pauses, perhaps for a drink of water.

"Teacher," the man asks politely, "what must I do to inherit eternal life?" Without hesitating, Jesus fires back a question. *Good tactics*, the lawyer thinks. Then he listens carefully as Jesus asks, "What is written in the Law? How do you read it?"

Wow, he's playing right into my strength. Okay, this answer will be good. "'Love the Lord your God with all your heart and with all your soul and with all your strength and with all your mind'; and 'Love your neighbor as yourself.'" *There, that ought to impress the crowd. It's the classical rabbinical summary of the Ten Commandments. What will Jesus say? There's no way he'll dare disagree.*

"You have answered correctly," Jesus replies. "Do this and you will live."

Wait just a minute. This isn't going quite the way I planned.

Then Jesus pins him to the wall with a look that shoots straight to the heart.

He knows! He knows I don't love God the way the Law demands. Nor do I love my neighbor as myself. What's left? Where do I go next? I know, I'll engage him in a technical debate over what Moses meant by neighbor. *This ought to be interesting. No country bumpkin can hold a candle to my trained mind.*

"Just who is my neighbor?" the lawyer asks.

Jesus responds by telling a story.

Instead of swallowing the bait, Jesus tells a story about a traveler whom thieves rob, nearly beat to death, and leave lying beside the road. A priest walks past, sees the wounded man, crosses the road, and keeps walking. Then a Levite, another religious type, does the same thing. Finally, a Samaritan—a despised social outcast—rides up the road on his donkey, sees the man, feels pity, and treats his wounds. Then the Samaritan hoists the injured man on his donkey, takes him to an inn, and cares for him. The following day, the Samaritan pays the innkeeper to look after the injured man and promises to reimburse extra costs.

As Jesus ends the story, he turns to his antagonist and asks,

"Which of these three do you think was a neighbor to the man who fell into the hands of robbers?"

There's no way out of this one. Even though it makes the priests and Levites look bad, the lawyer knows the right answer.

"The one who had mercy on him."

Now the teacher's eyes fix on him again. He feels the pressure as Jesus declares, "Go and do likewise."

That's it. Jesus turns away and starts a conversation with someone else. He dismisses the young lawyer to ponder the assignment he's been given.

As the lawyer reviews the conversation, it dawns on him that Jesus sent him a powerful message. Earlier in the day, the seventy-two disciples Jesus sent to preach the good news of the kingdom returned to report on their trips. The lawyer sensed their excitement about people from all walks of life responding to this message. He scoffed when they told Jesus that people repented of rebellion and found a home in the kingdom of God.

Yet the lawyer feels almost jealous.

This alarms him. He could lose way too much by letting this imposter influence him! He needs to maintain his reputation and build his career. Actually loving God and other people? Too messy and time-consuming. He needs to write a report and attend a strategy session. Next time he gets the chance, he won't be caught off guard. (For the whole story, see Luke 10:25–37.)

Formidable control issues protecting his personal kingdom explain the walls this temple lawyer has constructed. We don't know whether Jesus changes this man's attitude, but we can imagine his repentance. If he were to allow God to crack through his arrogant sense of superior intelligence and religious training, his attitude would change dramatically. Instead of just knowing the right answer, his life would reflect the reign of God. That kingdom exudes genuine love for others, contrasting sharply with a self-centered religious kingdom.

Sadly, this intellectual built a castle-of-the-heart like this:

The Expert in the Law
Luke 10:25–37

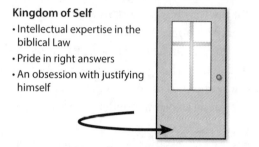

Kingdom of Self
- Intellectual expertise in the biblical Law
- Pride in right answers
- An obsession with justifying himself

Kingdom of God
You will live (eternally)

- "What must I do to inherit eternal life?"
- Move from knowing about to doing (vv. 28, 37)
- Give up your need to be superior
- Love God, love others (possible only when humble)

Still, self-important people can change. God can capture their attention in spite of intense resistance.

God can and does use intellect to draw people to himself.

A few years ago, Dr. Alex Thurman felt sure of himself. Since graduate school, he had taught freshman physics at a major West Coast university. His reputation as a faith-buster had grown steadily over the years. He loved teaching science, but even more, he thrived on debunking what he called "moronic religious beliefs." With a practiced technique, he punctured and sunk the faith of hundreds of students fresh from their hometowns, families, and churches. But then a student assistant got under his skin with the accuracy of her observations.

Ann was a beautiful woman with an intellect equal to his own. From the time she arrived to work for Alex two years before, he attempted to seduce her, without success. Because a long line of women willingly shared his bed through the years, he considered Ann's refusal a huge challenge to conquer. His last face-to-face conversation with her still haunts him.

Ann stood in his office, hands on her hips. "Alex," she said, "please accept the fact that you are not going to add me to your sad list of conquests. With all your urbane sophistication and cultured savvy, you see yourself as an eminently attractive—no, irresistible—man. I've watched your well-worn technique with amusement. It works too well. You select choice women from the year's new arrivals, shower them with flattering attention, offer them research jobs or some 'opportunity' that places you in daily contact, then you begin your skilled pursuit. Few hold out more than a month. You grant them sexual favors but gradually condition them to accept the fact it will be over when the research is finished or the college year is through."

"Ann"—the professor bristled—"how dare you caricature my private life! Where do you get off standing in judgment of my sex life?"

Ann laughed. "Caricature? Actually, I'm being kind. In two years I've watched you manipulate, use, and discard five women. At the same time, you've relentlessly pursued me. And there are at least a half dozen more women who have told me how you flattered and used them briefly, then moved on."

"So what?" he sputtered, furious with her critique. "Sex is a beautiful thing. I happen to find my satisfaction in loving many women."

"No!" Her anger now surpassed his. "You love no one but yourself. You subject everyone in your world to your insufferable ego, and you don't even notice or care about the damage you do, the pain you cause, and the lives you destroy. You've got it all rationalized and justified."

She sighed, glaring at the furious man behind his desk. "Alex, you act like God in your tiny little universe, but you are a deluded excuse for a human being. I can't even feel sorry for you. But I do feel sorry for all those you pollute with your arrogant superiority."

Ann opened the door and walked out . . . for good. She left her job. Just walked away. No one had ever dared talk to Alex like that. Then again, no one had ever been so accurate. He tried to evade the facts, but in more honest moments, he realized Ann spoke the truth.

Alex did not know what to do with this revelation. He started to suspect that what he had long considered the perfect life had degenerated into a world of invasive selfishness. Though he felt disoriented and lost, he pushed through it, trying to function as if nothing changed.

A few days later, a package from Ann arrived at his house. Inside, Alex found the book *Mere Christianity* by C. S. Lewis and a Bible. Enraged, he released a torrent of expletives and threw the books across the room. "Religion! What a cheap shot! I hate religion, especially Christianity." He stormed out of the house.

After his third trip around the block, he returned home, and eyed the books angrily. A paper had fallen out of one of the books and, against his better judgment, he picked it up and read:

Alex, The reason you are the way you are and deeply stuck there is because you have kicked God out and assumed his place in your universe. Grow up. In a few short years all your pseudo-intellectual defenses will come crashing down with a heart attack, a stroke, the big "C," or even AIDS, given your lifestyle. One thing I have to grant you: you do have a good brain. Use it. Listen to C. S. Lewis. He's got the things you mock and scorn figured out. As you like to say, "Ciao, baby." Ann

Alex picked up *Mere Christianity*. Unaware of time passing, he sat on his balcony and spent the rest of the day lost in a new world. Around midnight he finished the book, exhausted but convinced.

He struggled to admit he'd been wrong. Then he uttered his first real prayer. "God, I've been so wrong, and I've derailed a lot of people who believed in you. I don't know if there's hope for me, but if you'll have me after what I've done, I'm yours. Please help me understand you and what you want from me. I've built a whole worldview without you in it. I don't even know how to think about existence with you at the center. So show me, please?"

The next day Alex read the book again, and then started on the Bible. In two weeks he read it from cover to cover. He grew more convinced by the day. Finally he called Ann to thank her for the books.

"Is this some kind of a joke?" she asked, keeping her guard up.

"No, please listen to me," he begged. "I've read the book twice and just finished the whole Bible. Ann, I think I'm becoming a Christian, and I'm utterly miserable!"

"What? That's wonderful! That's the most unexpected answer to prayer I've ever received." After a long pause, she continued, "I think I know what's eating your insides. You're facing up to all the brave little skeptics, agnostics, and atheists you created through the years. Am I right?"

"Um, yes. I don't know if I'll ever be able to accept God's forgiveness for what I've done. What a colossal mistake I've made. I might as well have killed them."

In freshman physics Professor Thurman now enthralls his students with the beauty and incredible design evident in the universe. His appreciation for the planet and enthusiasm for exploring and preserving it are contagious. Inevitably a student remarks, "This planet and everything living on it screams intelligence. Are you aware this says there must be a God?"

Then the professor talks about his personal journey. He concludes by saying, "Each of you must make up your own mind on these important matters. All I can say is, from where I stand now, I think you have to deliberately misread and misinterpret the facts to disregard the obvious. I once manipulated the data to make sure

I would arrive at my preselected conclusion. I wanted a cosmos without God. That was the best way to set myself up in his place and run my life to please myself. It worked for a long time. I built a world of blindness that I was convinced was sight. You have that option in front of you as well. I beg you to stay with the facts, not the politically correct versions of science.

"Physics is all about order and design. About laws that govern the forces making up our universe. We didn't create them. We just discovered them and learned how to use them. It is now my humble opinion that when you have laws, you have a lawgiver. When you have overwhelming evidence of intelligent design, you have an intelligent designer. Unless such a conclusion gets in the way of your personal autonomy and career."

Chaos can seem like freedom.

The kingdom of the mind constructs a powerful fortress to fight God's invasion. Perhaps the toughest walls to crack represent science, the modern alternative to religion. Schools of thought like evolution, humanism, naturalism, and rationalism combine forces to create a powerful, illusionary vision of a universe devoid of God.

In this worldview, the obsession with self-centered kingdom-building thrives. It eliminates the challenge of accountability to a higher authority. We scramble to the top of the heap and attempt to control one another. And who feels better qualified to lead than the intellectual elite?

It seems like freedom: the brave new world; the great society; the new-world order. Yet without the framework of restraint and safety provided by God's government, the situation logically degenerates into "every person for themselves." Survival of the most ambitious, strong, intelligent, and ruthless. This creates a war-like environment: billions of conflicting, colliding agendas with no hope for lasting peace or escape. Chaos.

In my opinion, the so-called scientific century—the twentieth century—was the bloodiest and most violent in history. With ever more destructive weapons we continued our ancient pattern of warfare. MAD (mutual assured destruction) was the only thing holding us in check . . . barely. Intellectual enlightenment did not solve our biggest problems.

Living without God, eliminating him, feels intellectually intoxicating, but it's personally messy and corporately dangerous. If you are beginning to realize this, now might be the opportunity to investigate genuine intellectual freedom. Consider the possibility of not caving in to political correctness. Think independently. Compare the kingdom of God with the kingdoms even the smartest people build. Be spiritually intelligent. God loves intelligence. He created it. He always welcomes the questions of a good mind.

FIVE

ANGRY WITH GOD

Clarissa reveled in her angry role as a church dropout. Her parents practiced their faith mostly through church attendance. Since infancy she attended Sunday school, children's church, and youth group. Then at age seventeen, she watched in horror as her best girlfriend faced the congregation for disciplinary action. Clarissa's friend had gotten pregnant by a guy from the wrestling team. When the friend could no longer cover up the obvious, she confessed to the youth pastor and her parents. For Clarissa, that's when things turned ugly.

The girls' conservative evangelical church took sin seriously. The leaders insisted the friend confess her sin to the congregation and ask for forgiveness. Outraged, Clarissa took up a huge offense for her friend and lashed out in a furious attack on the church leaders and the youth pastor. Oddly enough, her friend did not react the same way. Humble and repentant, she confessed her sin. This inflamed Clarissa even more.

As social media developed, Clarissa researched websites and blogs of people also angry with their churches. Soon she learned a new language of disdain. She called her church "abusive" and "toxic." She shared her anger, and it grew. The stories she heard from others confirmed her crusade's validity. Based on this interaction, obviously churches were dangerous groups who harmed more than helped.

Eventually Clarissa stopped attending church. Her parents tried to reason with her, but she considered them brainwashed, participating in a cover-up of injustice. After college she married and had a couple of kids. But still, if someone mentioned Christianity or church, she released a torrent of rage and disgust as if her disappointment happened yesterday. She called all religion hypocritical and abusive.

Ironically, Clarissa's former girlfriend, now married, stayed deeply involved at the church where they grew up. She felt heartsick about Clarissa's enmity against churches and, ultimately, God. She prayed for Clarissa and tried to stay in touch despite consistent rebuffs. Clarissa denied her friend's experience of forgiveness, acceptance, and compassion within the church community. In her view, the former friend's love for a church family encompassed victimhood within a sick system of abuse, oppression, and codependency.

When Clarissa's husband, Bob, contacted me, he looked broken. He said Clarissa had kicked him out of their home, again, for the offense of challenging her about out-of-control anger. He still loved his wife but found it impossible to live with her.

"She will not stand for any disagreement. Disagreeing with her is considered abuse or mistreatment," he said. "She will tolerate me as long as I never question her choices, attitudes, or opinions. If I dare to confront Clarissa, she immediately flies into a rage and demands that I leave."

"How are your children doing?" I asked.

Bob grimaced and tears brimmed. Then he explained. "Our oldest, Trish, just turned fourteen. She is strong willed like her mother. The problem is she is just as angry as her mother, or maybe even more so. I'm actually afraid they will try to kill each other, if it gets that out of control."

"Is there anybody in Clarissa's life that she respects and to whom she might listen?" I asked.

"No, certainly no one from the Christian community would be tolerated. The one person she seems to trust is her therapist, but that's because he tells her what she wants to hear."

"Okay," I said. "Let's begin to pray for God to bring someone into her life that she will trust and hear at the level of this old grudge that's twisting her into knots." And that's what we did. We met weekly for prayer. We fasted and prayed, and God answered in a startling way.

Clarissa found a lump in her breast. Her doctor referred her to a specialist who diagnosed it as cancer. To my amazement, the specialist was a woman of great and bold faith. During the cancer treatment, surgery, and recovery, Clarissa heard from God through her physician. This doctor compassionately, firmly, and biblically addressed her patient's anger. After listening to her story, the physician told Clarissa she lived in deliberate disobedience to God. She even suggested that Clarissa's attitude toward the church and the way she rationalized it was serious sin. She also advised Clarissa that her chance of recovery would improve if she got rid of the internal stress caused by bitterness.

Finally, an authority in Clarissa's life—someone she respected—captured her attention. But it also required the fear of death to move her to action. I would not say God gave Clarissa a serious illness to get her attention. But he does use illness or difficult circumstances to open doors to otherwise closed hearts.

Forgiveness is never easy, and Clarissa agonized over letting her offense go. But in the end she called her former pastor and requested to meet with him and the church board. She wanted to apologize and ask for forgiveness. Clarissa decided she harbored a secondhand offense. Through malicious talk, she had repeatedly tried to destroy the church leaders. Now she felt genuinely sorry, and to their credit, the leaders accepted the apology and forgave her.

Clarissa's husband says the days afterward felt like living with a new wife. The bitter anger simply disappeared and gentleness developed in its place. (Of course, change was a process and Clarissa sometimes regressed to old habits. Forgiveness started with a decision and then became many choices, a way of life.) Still feisty and opinionated, Clarissa struck a deal with her daughter to work together on controlling their mutual bent toward taking offense. So far it seems this agreement is working remarkably well.

The dark side to Christmas reveals why we need a savior.

The New Testament opens with the carpenter Joseph's despair over Mary, his betrothed. She's pregnant, but not by him. After Jesus's birth, the story moves quickly to royal visitors from the East arriving in Jerusalem, and the horrific violence of King Herod as he removes threats to his throne. The king, in his paranoia, had already murdered his wife and a son. Now hearing the ancient prophecy about a Messiah, he commands the murder of all baby boys, two years old and younger, living in Bethlehem's vicinity. He will not allow rivals, especially not God's promised Messiah (see Matt. 1:18–2:18). Why would God start the story of his Son's birth with so dark and depressing an account?

Recently I spoke at a Christmas banquet at the huge reformatory in Monroe, Washington. At the dinner I spoke to 150 inmates and their relatives about "The Dark Side of Christmas" found in Matthew's gospel. I suggested that God begins the story of Jesus's birth with the murder of the innocents because he wants to put in place the reason we all need a Savior.

Jesus, later in his life, describes his mission on earth as coming to seek and save those who were lost (Luke 19:10). Lost like King Herod and lost like all of us.

Few of us have killed another human in cold blood. But Jesus says this three decades after his birth: "You have heard that it was said to the people long ago, 'You shall not murder, and anyone who murders will be subject to judgment.' But I tell you that anyone who is angry with his brother or sister will be subject to judgment" (Matt. 5:21–22). Jesus places murder and anger in the same category because anger turns into hate, and hate into violence, and violence into murder. Accumulated or stored anger turns into rage. The older anger grows, the more toxic it becomes and the more likely it results in words and actions precipitating harm, pain, and death.

After the prison banquet a middle-aged inmate approached me with an awkward smile. "I thought at first your talk was going to be a real downer. But as you went on I realized it was the best Christmas message I've ever heard."

"Glad you liked it," I said. "But what changed your mind?"

"If you had to live in here you'd know the truth of what you said from hard experience. This place is a powder keg of anger. Almost everybody here is offended with someone. Many are bitter and angry at a level that's hard to fathom. In fact, out-of-control anger is what got most of us locked up in the first place. Society wouldn't put up with the extent of our rage and the destructive ways we acted it out."

Pensively, I answered, "Sir, sad to say, it isn't much different outside, as I'm sure you would guess. A huge number of people in the culture are like time bombs waiting for the right combination of circumstances to go off. Most of the time they blow up their marriages and families or their personal health or finances with their anger and bitterness. But Jesus came to offer a better way to live. His forgiveness gives those who receive it the incentive to also forgive."

"I get that," he said. "I just don't think I will ever be able to forgive my father. He doesn't deserve forgiveness. I don't know if even God could forgive him."

"Do you think you can be forgiven?" I asked.

It was as if I had struck him. He shook his head and stepped back, frowning. I saw in his eyes the sudden realization that he and his father occupied the same boat. I then pursued the happy but risky task of explaining neither of them deserved forgiveness. But Jesus loved them enough to take their place and die for the consequences their sins deserved. He wanted to forgive them, if they would ask.

"I guess that was the whole point of your talk tonight, wasn't it? I'm just not ready for it yet," he said.

Looking back, we can see that the prisoner and Clarissa both built walls of anger and unforgiveness. This kind of interior castle seems like an impressive position of strength. Eventually it tends to become a fortress that challenges and keeps at bay the kingdom of God. Both of these angry people found someone to blame and condemn as a means of justifying chronic rage. One of them let down the drawbridge through forgiveness; the other built higher defenses.

Jesus tells a story about two brothers.

Upon first reading, the Parable of the Prodigal Son (Luke 15:11–32) seems to be about the youngest son who throws away his inheritance on wild living and then returns home in repentance to a loving, forgiving father. But on a deeper level, at the heart of Jesus's redemptive message lies the return of prodigal sons and daughters and God's grace in receiving them back.

The prodigal son has an older brother, the one who remains home. He seems like the "good son," the hard-working, responsible one. Unlike his younger brother, he doesn't ask for an early inheritance. Yet when the wayward brother returns and receives forgiveness, the good son boils into a rage. He takes major offense when his father lets the pathetic little beggar back into the family.

He feels affronted by an unworthy sibling receiving a celebration feast. The older brother says to his father,

"Listen, all these years I've worked hard for you. I've never disobeyed one of your orders. But how many times have you even given me a little goat to roast for a party with my friends? Not once! This is not fair! So this son of yours comes, this wasteful delinquent who has spent your hard-earned wealth on loose women, and what do you do? You butcher the fattest calf from our herd!"

The father replied, "My son, you are always with me, and all I have is yours. Isn't it right to join in the celebration and be happy? This is your brother we're talking about. He was dead and is alive again; he was lost and is found again!" (vv. 29–32 VOICE)

Jesus never finishes the story. As it ends, the older brother feels angry and resentful. He begrudges his father for his extravagant mercy and forgiveness. Unless he recants this attitude, self-pity and bitterness will undoubtedly contaminate the relationship with his father and brother for the rest of his life.

Bitterness and anger have no part in God's kingdom.

In our global entertainment culture, a significant part of popular novels, TV shows, and movies feature an unjustly injured person exacting revenge on an enemy. Universally accepted clichés claim, "Revenge is sweet," and "Revenge is a dish best served cold." Getting even is the norm. In the real world we may not shoot or stab our enemies, but we eagerly trash reputations and destroy credibility with words. And it seems like the acceptable, even necessary thing to do.

Look around. Liberals relentlessly assault conservatives and, in turn, conservatives attack liberals. Radical Muslims terrorize the world in the name of jihad and as payback for the Crusades, a grudge eight hundred years old. Americans go to war with Iraq and Afghanistan in reaction to the terrorist attacks on 9/11 in which 3,000 people died. Women feel offended by men and vice versa. Blacks retaliate for the old wound of white domination, the poor resent the rich, and evolutionists tear apart creationists. Young and old play violent video games. Revenge seems like the air we breathe. We're constantly offended and ready to make somebody pay.

In contrast, Jesus emphasizes the path to God's forgiveness winds through the difficult terrain of forgiving others. This is radical, unexpected, and countercultural. His famous model prayer states, "Forgive us our debts, as we also have forgiven our debtors" (Matt. 6:12). Apparently, God will forgive our wrongs against him if we forgive those who wronged us. Immediately following this prayer Jesus explains, "If you forgive other people when they sin against you, your heavenly Father will also forgive you. But if you do not forgive others their sins, your Father will not forgive your sins" (vv. 14–15).

If, after receiving forgiveness, we persist in revenge and an obsession with personal justice, nobody can depend on us as safe and reliable citizens of God's kingdom. We would disturb even the peace of heaven with our anger and thirst for revenge. Still, God extends his marvelous forgiveness to us. He freely and completely forgives all who admit they need it and who willingly begin a lifestyle of forgiveness.

It's possible to be forgiven but unforgiving.

The first followers of Jesus struggle with the idea of forgiveness as a way of life. They suggest that forgiving an offender seven times is a huge stretch. Jesus says seventy-seven times is more like it (Matt. 18:21–22). The disciples seem to think limitless forgiveness is too difficult. So Jesus does what he does so well; he tells a story that clarifies the issues:

> Think about a king who wanted to settle accounts with his servants. Just as the king began to get his accounts in order, his assistants called his attention to a slave who owed a huge sum to him—what a laborer might make in 500 lifetimes. The slave, maybe an embezzler, had no way to make restitution, so the king ordered that he, his wife, their children, and everything the family owned be sold on the auction block; the proceeds from the slave sale would go toward paying back the king. Upon hearing this judgment, the slave fell down, prostrated himself before the king, and begged for mercy: "Have mercy on me, and I will somehow pay you everything." The king was moved by the pathos of the situation, so indeed he took pity on the servant, told him to stand up, and then forgave the debt. (vv. 23–27 VOICE)

Jesus then gets to the issue of forgiveness, when the forgiven slave refuses to give a fellow slave the kind of treatment he had received himself. Apparently, the forgiven slave was owed a fairly small amount but threw his debtor into prison. People watching were incensed. They saw it as very wrong for someone who had been forgiven so much to refuse to pass it on. They reported his behavior to the king.

That ugly picture of the slave's querulous behavior shocked the king, and in anger he rescinded his decision to forgive the slave. In the end, the unforgiving slave is in a much worse situation than when the story began.

Who fits this profile?

If God forgives us through Jesus's sacrificial death, no matter what we have or haven't done, then the unmerciful servant story holds profound implications. It could mean many people refuse God's forgiveness because they won't forgive those who offend them. When we say yes to Jesus and accept forgiveness, we need to think seriously about "paying it forward." Clarissa eventually did. Herod and the prodigal's brother did not.

It's challenging. I struggle with this idea. I carry a well-developed sense of justice that wants to right all wrongs. Forgiveness seems too easy, maybe even cheap, given the seriousness of some offenses. But when I realize how much forgiveness cost God, I know it isn't cheap. In fact, it's the only way to a new world free from constant conflict, prolonged war, and endless payback.

Human history reeks of conflict. A tour of England and Europe isn't complete without visits to the numerous ruins of castles crumbling into dust. Those old fortresses worked well to protect kings and queens, princes and lords in their day. Today's weapons make them obsolete. Now we take shelter in bunkers of hardened concrete and steel built deep underground to withstand nuclear bombs. But the realities of human nature are the same. The inner bunkers we build seem necessary for protecting ourselves, even though they're constructed from the ugly stuff of prejudice, dogmatism, bigotry, segregation, enmity, and hatred.

As long as people build personal kingdoms of offense, anger, unforgiveness, or revenge, the world will be restless and dangerous. Our nations and families will feel unsafe. If we don't forgive, we refuse God's offer of a peaceable kingdom, a place free from offense and payback. We miss the chance to enter the door to a paradise that Jesus opened at incredible cost. That is a high price to pay for living in kingdoms of retribution.

SIX

BLAMING GOD

Bad things happen. Nobody gets out of this life without a share of pain. What we choose to do with our pain determines whether we open ourselves to God's touch.

The victim mentality often stands in opposition to God's kingdom. This alternate kingdom appears as an unavoidable and unfair condition of damage, brokenness, and helplessness. But according to Jesus, it's not always what it seems. When Jesus meets a lame, victimized man, he feels compassion, but he also pinpoints an underlying cause for the chronic disability. He exposes a mentality contributing to the man's long-term suffering.

Jesus encounters a lame man.

Jesus approaches the chronically ill man, who is lying with a multitude of inflicted people under the porches of the pool of Bethesda, near the Sheep Gate of Jerusalem. The blind, lame, paralyzed, and other seriously sick or disabled people gather near the pool because of its reputation. Legend claims an angel periodically stirs up the water, and the first person to next step into the pool will be healed. The pool represents hope, a last resort for despairing people.

The Bible doesn't explain why Jesus picks this particular man, disabled for thirty-eight years, out of the crowd. After years of failed attempts to dip into the healing pool, he waits for another angelic stirring of the water. Jesus knows the man's condition and history, but still asks, "Do you want to get well?"

The sick man answers, "Sir, I have no one to help me into the pool when the water is stirred. While I am trying to get in, someone else goes down ahead of me."

Jesus's answer indicates that the years of lonely self-pity can cease. Someone cares. "Get up! Pick up your mat and walk."

It's startling to see the response. No questioning look, no incredulity. Immediately, the man gets to his feet, rolls up his mat, and walks.

This happens on the Sabbath day, and Jewish leaders get upset when they see the healed man carrying his bedroll. In their minds, this activity is not permissible on the Sabbath. They demand the name of the one who broke the law by healing him. The man tells them what happened, but can't help with the identity of his benefactor. He simply does not know who healed him.

Later Jesus finds the formerly lame man in the temple and says, "See, you are well again. Stop sinning or something worse may happen to you." (See John 5:1–15.)

Beware of a connection between illness and sin.

From my perspective as a caregiver, this man's chronic condition indicates what persists in his heart more than his legs. When the lame man tells Jesus his excuse for not reaching the pool in time, I think he inadvertently exposes a spirit of blame and self-pity. In effect, he says, "My condition is not my fault; I have no one to help me." But in a crowd of people this doesn't make sense. If he is friendly and concerned for the needs of others, he might find the help he needs. People with a woe-is-me mind-set quickly wear out their potential caregivers and wind up alone.

"I'll help you, then next time you help me," could be a successful formula for the lame man. Instead, oblivious to other people's pain, he wallows in lonely misery. In fact, he labels other sick people as competition ("While I am trying to get in, someone else goes down ahead of me."), not fellow sufferers or friends in the same fix. This man builds an inner kingdom of victimization, abandoned by God and people.

Generally speaking, living as a victim creates a special-case identity. It's clever, allowing someone to live as an exception to the relational rules of God and society. A victim often builds walls of anger, complaint, criticism, and bitterness, shutting out others. A victim unintentionally drives off the love and support he craves. And these seemingly protective behaviors can contribute to health problems. An attempt to build a kingdom of victimhood can easily make somebody sick.

If I'm right about this mental fortress, it explains why Jesus asks the disabled man the curious question, "Do you want to get well?"

I'm surprised the sick man doesn't swing a crutch at Jesus and shout, "Stop making fun of me! Of course I want to get well. Why do you think I have been lying here all these years? I'm certainly not sunbathing!"

Jesus reveals the biggest clue to this disability when he deliberately seeks the healed man in the temple. In their second encounter, the Lord delivers a direct warning: "Stop sinning or something worse may happen to you" (v. 14). This is a diagnostic statement. It connects choices to health.

Jesus knows the man's heart and what set him up for wasted years. I'm quite certain he refers to the sin of justifying anger and bitterness toward God and people. Such a spiritual condition creates a special-case identity. The "victim" classifies himself as an exception and not required to act like other people. Jesus diagnoses the cause of his previous condition as sin, and the prognosis says his health problems will return if he repeats the same kind of behavior.

What kind of sin pattern could so powerfully grip a partially paralyzed elderly man? Lust? Greed? Stealing? My guess is chronic self-pity and bitterness. This kind of sin can throw the immune system off-balance and initiate dysfunction at the body's weakest point. He probably appears to others as a person who lacks room for anyone but himself.

The Paralyzed Victim
John 5:1–15

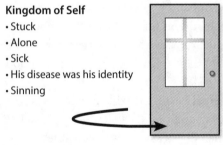

Kingdom of Self
- Stuck
- Alone
- Sick
- His disease was his identity
- Sinning

Kingdom of God
- "Stop sinning," Jesus told him
- Told others Jesus made him well

- Sought by Jesus
- Rose, took up his bed, and walked
- Healed
- Obeyed Jesus

Thankfully, Jesus doesn't ignore negative, self-focused people. In this fascinating story, he grants new life to a man who couldn't supply help for himself. Then in response to this unexpected generosity, the man obeys Jesus immediately! With a sudden burst of crazy faith, he jumps up without delay, picks up his mat, and walks. He expresses faith with instant obedience.

The lame man's story represents the way God's kingdom often arrives. One minute we're stuck in sin—our restless kingdom of "me," our self-induced hopelessness—and the next, the gospel showers us with grace. We receive the God-given ability to repent, believe, and obey. In turn, when we allow God's reign in our lives, life-giving benefits accompany him. It's not the same for everybody. Often inner healing results, yet sometimes both inner and outer healing occur simultaneously. When an old, negative kingdom of the heart is exchanged for the new management of Jesus, positive changes occur.

The power of the victim role is hard to resist.

A friend commented to me, "In the modern cultures of western civilization, the system is set up so the victim has all the power." At the time we discussed a married couple we knew. Both husband and wife claimed victim status as a means of getting more out of the divorce settlement. Not long after that, I was reintroduced to a true professional victim.

Carol considered herself a victim of male chauvinism, injustice, the "system," and bad luck. She could not carry on a conversation without lashing out at somebody. I met her again when she entered my church looking for a handout. When the receptionist asked Carol to fill out a financial assistance form, she emotionally hit the roof. Her cursing and loud, angry attack on our receptionist brought me running from my office.

I introduced myself, and immediately she raged at me with spit flying, arms waving, and tears coursing down her grimy cheeks.

She screamed, "You people make me sick! You call yourselves Christians but you are nothing but self-righteous frauds. You are supposed to take care of the poor and the abused victims of society, but no, you couldn't care less! I came here asking for help and what do I get? Another piece of paper to fill out to prove I am who I say I am and that I'm really in need. This is sick! You are all a bunch of hypocrites!" At that point she broke down and sat on the floor, head in her hands, sobbing hysterically.

By this time I recognized Carol and even remembered her name. I knew her as a professional con artist who scammed churches in the region. It was her "job." She developed a circuit, hitting the northwest religious community for handouts over the summer months, heading south in the fall, and working California churches during the winter. My staff tracked her and several others by comparing notes with various churches. Each year her costume looked different—she always changed her hair color—and she told a new sob story with amazingly creative details. Carol was a professional street person, but she never lived in homeless shelters or ate in soup kitchens. She considered herself too good a performer to live as what she called a "bottom-feeder."

One year, when Carol arrived either high or drunk or both, she had slipped and admitted to one of my fellow pastors that some years she earned as much as $50,000, tax free! As churches caught on to her and others, our staff developed forms and tracking procedures, making it difficult for con artists to fool us. Carol hated this process, and it set off her latest rant. After she calmed down and we talked, she candidly said we made it much harder for her to make a living. It wasn't fair that we no longer served as easy marks.

I asked, "Carol, why don't you stop living a lie and put your obvious talents to work in a legitimate way? God has given you some amazing abilities!"

That set off an unprintable tirade. She talked for the next hour, enumerating the bad things that had happened over her lifetime, and why she deserved victim status. She believed society owed her everything she conned out of it. She thought God required Christians to take care of her, even if she deceived them with a shtick. She felt entitled to everything she got.

As I listened to Carol expertly claim the high ground of victimhood, I once again thought about human kingdom building. We ingeniously and creatively set up and control our personal kingdoms, even if we build on foundations of negative pride. Carol definitely thought she was the righteous one in the room. Her beat-up ego sounded just as arrogant and proud as any self-made business tycoon. Her sense of injustice and beliefs about what the world owed her could not be even moderately penetrated with truth, much like people who make it to the top of the economic ladder.

And yet I knew God loved Carol, and he filled me with compassion and tenderness for her. I carefully explained the gospel of God's love in Jesus. I told her the good news: all the shameful things could be forgiven and removed from her record forever. I remembered sharing the same message with her several years before. She'd heard the Christian salvation message many times as she worked the churches, but I tried again.

Stony-eyed, she said, "Just cut the crap. I've heard that baloney a thousand times. Are you going to give me some money or not? I am sick and tired of having to 'Come to Jesus' for a few bucks."

"No, Carol, I am not going to give you any money," I said. "I will drive you to the nearest homeless shelter, and I will give you a coupon for a wholesome meal at a local restaurant within walking distance. But no money, because I know you still have your addictions. I can smell the alcohol on you. You've probably been drinking since you got up this morning. I won't contribute to your destruction, but I will try to help you."

That set off the most profane explosion of the afternoon. When her rage finally drained away, she wearily asked, "Why can't you people just let me go to hell without trying to stand in my way?"

As she gathered up energy to storm out the door, I pleaded, "Carol, that's the problem with love. It doesn't give up and it doesn't let go. Please stop running away and let God love you!" Then she disappeared into the dusk of a descending night.

Jesus knows who is ready.

I believe Jesus picks the man lying beside the pool of Bethesda because he is ready to relinquish a kingdom of bitterness, self-pity, and victimhood. That's why Jesus walks past others just as sick, just as needy, and just as hopeless. The lame man lets Jesus tell him what to do, and he obeys immediately.

The Spirit of God searches the earth to find pliable, obedient hearts. The Creator wants to guide us, not just boss us around. His goal is freeing us from the paralysis of sin. How we respond to Jesus's question, "Do you want to get well?" is a critical, life-changing turning point.

Carol told me and God to get lost, to leave her alone so she could go to hell in her own way. That's a tragic expression of the kingdom of victimhood. But we can follow the man by the pool instead, responding to Jesus immediately. We can let our self-made walls crumble. We can stop blaming God for our own choices and ask him to exchange his kingdom for ours.

SEVEN

ABUSING GOD

Jason Carter is a very smart twentysomething. He slammed through college and now conquers graduate school in a near record blitz of effort and intelligence. He operates on a conviction that the smartest people figure out who is the authority in any given situation, learn the group's rules, and comply with them both. To live successfully, his bottom line rests on winning by complying.

However, something inside Jason shifted when he started working on a PhD. He began wondering about the validity of the personal convictions propelling him to excel with honors and top awards through his schooling so far.

Jason knows his perspective puts him at odds with the prevailing views of his teachers and other students. The campus abounds with messages insisting that breaking rules and defying authorities constitute the basic obligation of intelligence and freedom. Many of his friends choose self-assertion that destroys their health, relationships, and potential in the job market. Instead of recognizing this sabotage, they practice victimhood, playing the unfairness card at every turn.

When Jason tries to confront his friends about the foolishness of rebellion and defiance as a lifestyle strategy, they jeer and mock him. The grad students in his dorm simply point to their professors, the most intelligent people they know. "Don't you hear what they're telling us? Authorities are the enemy. Rules are how the authorities control us and keep us working for them! The system is unfair and must be broken down so a new world can be put in its place."

Jason retorts, "Okay, try getting a passing grade in one of their classes by practicing that philosophy. They will slap you down just as fast as any other authority on the planet. Don't you get it? Exhorting people to defy authority is only acceptable and noble when it's someone else's authority, not theirs, that's being challenged."

Sometimes Jason despairs over the waste of time and effort he sees as others reject authority. He can only assume somebody is crazy: him or his schoolmates. He knows his view of the way the system works must be right. He just doesn't know why it's right or who decides the way things work.

Jason now manages his new business start-up while finishing his PhD dissertation. He loves the rush of excitement from these challenges. Yet he still questions why he stands alone in his personal philosophy.

Are intelligent people always right?

I met Jason through a mutual friend and we immediately discovered much in common. When Jason described his personal philosophy on the best way to live, it shocked me. I know few Christians who could articulate so accurate a biblical view. But when I asked if he operated his life in the same fashion outside of professional education, he looked genuinely puzzled.

"What do you mean?" he asked.

"Do you figure out the authority structure in all the other compartments of your life—like government, business, family, and religion—and work within the rules there, too?"

His eyes brightened and excitement surfaced.

"Yes. The answer is yes!" he said, nodding his head vigorously. "It was actually my father who taught me the shortest path to success was through working with the system, not against it. Apparently, I was a hardhead when I was young and pushed against his authority."

I probed further. "What is your relationship like with your Dad now?"

"My parents see eye to eye with me on this philosophy in every area of life, except religion," Jason said, his face growing solemn and his voice soft.

He gauged the interest in my face and continued. "We don't agree there is a God. I have sort of outgrown the church scene. My parents still hold to a pattern of personal faith and church attendance and involvement. It has always been very important to them. In recent years it's become a topic where we've agreed to disagree, although both of them still bring it up quite often. I know I've hurt and disappointed them by rejecting that part of the way they raised me."

"I would be interested in hearing how you arrived at the conclusion that your dad was right in most things but wrong in his commitment to God," I responded.

"It should be obvious to any educated person. I'm surprised you would even ask. The smartest people I've met in my education process have all concluded the idea of God is unnecessary and, in fact, an obstacle to science and rational thinking," he answered.

"Are these intelligent people always right?"

"Frankly, I ask myself that question often," he said. "They seem to be crazy smart about a lot of things but really ignorant about others. Like my principle of figuring out who's in charge and what the rules are in any given situation. All my instructors and my peers, except for one guy, think I'm the one with brain damage.

They almost universally accept personal autonomy when it comes to God. I would actually call it a kind of spiritual anarchy, but they are adamant that such a philosophy is the best way for educated people to live. Questioning authority and throwing off the rules of God and man is viewed as necessary, except in the arena of their personal field of expertise. There they bow and scrape to the reigning experts in the most abject fashion."

"Give me an example," I said.

"Okay, let's take the field of biology. You simply can't get anywhere in the realm of science if you question anything about evolution. It is as sacred to the secular mind as the Bible is to the Christian mind. So what I'm saying is that I've observed this weird mix of personal independence from authority and almost slavish compliance to authority in the same people. It's really confusing."

"I see your point," I replied, "but what has this to do with you being on a different wavelength from your parents when it comes to God?"

"Maybe what I'm saying, and I've never admitted this out loud before, is that I can't afford to believe in God. Remember, I'm a pragmatist. I figure out how things work in any given situation and try to get on the good side of how it works. The 'good side' in the world of higher education has no room for God. In fact, believing in God has a serious downside. You get locked into a freak category unless you hide your religious convictions. I have found it much easier to excel in the environment I'm in by not dragging along the baggage of my religious upbringing."

Jason hesitated for a long moment, and then said, "I know that sounds a bit cowardly or even like a kind of betrayal, but I have found it is foolish to spit into the wind of the way things are in the real world."

I feel great empathy for Jason and young adults in today's universities and colleges. They obviously encounter high hoops to jump through that previous generations did not. So I carefully approached the crucial question we needed to discuss.

"Do you mind if I ask you about the religious baggage you have chosen to discard?"

He smiled and nodded. "Okay. I know I'm inconsistent in that area but I'm willing to go there."

I shifted. "Let's frame the issue by returning to your principle for achieving success. Do you still believe in God?"

"Which god?" he shot back.

"Fair question," I replied. "How about starting with the God of your parents, the Christian deity they raised you to believe in?"

Jason fell silent for a while. Then he admitted with regret, "Okay, yes, I still have some belief that God exists. I cannot bring myself to deny that my parents' faith has made them better people. They live a very beautiful and peace-filled life. My dad and mom do not think of themselves first. They are generous to a fault and give to anyone in their life circle who has a real need. I am probably the first in line when it comes to receiving their generosity. I don't think they would be so self-donating and others-oriented if they had a pretend God.

"On the other hand, the people I've met since I left home have made it clear that putting themselves first is common sense. I've observed that most of them either don't believe in God or, like me, have suspended their belief. So I guess maybe a strong belief in God makes a better person out of you in some cases. But then again, there are the horrible things people do in the name of devout religious beliefs that are part of what makes our world such a dangerous place. Everybody knows extremely religious people invented modern terrorism. That makes it easy to justify not believing, or only believing minimally. Can you see where I'm coming from?"

"Of course. You are impacted by some tragic behavioral realities, as are we all," I said. "In my judgment, you are wise to hesitate before throwing the baby out with the bathwater. Could we return to your original idea that it is wise to figure out who is in charge in any given situation and what they expect from you?"

"Sure," he answered.

"What if the true God, the original Creator of everything, is indeed the God of the Bible? What if he gave humans the freedom to choose either him or themselves? What if the twistedness in religion originates from people choosing to go their own way and create their own form of religion? What if many religious people are trying to compensate for the emptiness or restlessness they feel inside or as a way to appease their sense of guilt?"

It was a lot to ask, but strangely enough, he considered my questions reasonable.

"I suspect you are going after the big weakness in how I live given my personal philosophy, right? Believe me, I know I am violating my own principle of compliance with authority when it comes to God," he said. "I actually feel a bit apprehensive about what I just referred to as suspending my belief in God. It seemed to me more of a choice between authorities, with God coming out on the short end of the stick."

I countered, "And if God is there and not a figment of feverish imaginations, aren't you taking the biggest risk possible?"

I sensed Jason's conflict. He treated God differently from other authorities. It seemed a good possibility he wanted to close that glaring gap.

Jason thought about my question for several minutes, started to say something a couple of times, but kept thinking. Finally, he said, "The reason I have been telling people that I'm an agnostic and don't know if there is a God is because I can't reconcile my own internal contradiction. If I say I believe in God, but don't allow him to have a God-sized role in my life, I am a hypocrite. It's been easier to assume the agnostic position, but it does have a price tag . . . restlessness." At that point, Jason glanced at his watch and thanked me for taking time to talk with him. He said he needed to meet a friend but wanted to have another conversation with me.

We set up another time and Jason left on his mountain bike, daypack full of books and thesis chapters strapped to his back.

Privilege can create a significant problem.

The next time we met, Jason closed his heart, unwilling to pick up our conversation where we left it. He offered no explanation. His previous openness seemed unreal, the difference in his manner pronounced. Jason reminded me of Pilate, the Roman governor in the New Testament. His conflict between inner knowledge of Jesus and the demands of those rejecting him as the Messiah eventually shut down his soul.

According to the historical record, Pilate tries to establish Jesus's identity. Jewish authorities pressure him to condemn Jesus to death for heresy, but Pilate cannot get his head around the issue. All four gospel writers record his pre-crucifixion conversation. Each one writes a unique version of the interaction between Jesus and Pilate (see Matt. 27:11–26; Mark 15:1–15; Luke 22:66–23:25; John 18:28–19:16).

Both pragmatic men, Jason and Pilate understand the high value of working within the system, and yet feel susceptible to peer pressure and groupthink.

Jason learns about Jesus from his parents. Pilate questions Jesus personally. Jason rejects Jesus because of inconvenience. He finds it difficult to stand up to people's opinions. Pilate hears Jesus confess he is the King of the Jews. He also hears the Jewish leaders charge Jesus with blasphemy for calling himself the Son of God. Pilate knows Jesus proves innocent of the charges against him. Yet to satisfy the demands of Jewish leaders and an assembled mob, he hands Jesus over for crucifixion.

Pilate even receives a supernatural warning through his wife. She sends word of her haunting dream about Jesus. Claudia begs her husband, "Don't have anything to do with that innocent man, for I have suffered a great deal today in a dream because of him" (Matt. 27:19). She believes God sent her a warning. Pilate ignores the message.

The Cynical Politician: *Pilate*
Matthew 27:11–26

Kingdom of Self
- A man of power and politics
- Knew Jesus was innocent
- Heard Jesus say he was King

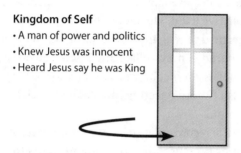

Kingdom of God
- Could have believed
- Could have done what was right
- Could have become a "God fearer"

Jason witnesses a father and mother who cultivate a personal relationship with Jesus. They live their relationship with God with consistency before Jason, especially when raising him in their home. He admits their testimony is powerful and convincing. But Jesus embarrasses him. Religion is a liability in his world of higher education. So, like Pilate, Jason goes along with the crowd, rejecting Jesus rather than standing up for him.

Some things never change.

If our football team is stopped one yard away from the goal line when time runs out, or we're one of two people being considered for a job and it's offered to the other candidate, we say, "So close, and yet so far!" Missing something by inches or minutes disappoints us. But missing a life connection with God by making a calculated choice to go on alone comprises a more serious matter.

Jason's decision to step away from his tried-and-true operating principle, getting on the good side, sounds sensible to most people. Why would anyone give up control to an ultimate authority when conventional wisdom says we can be "spiritual" without so radical a move? The vast majority of people, including Christians, seem to get along fine by bowing to cultural peer pressure rather than to God. Nominal or minimalist Christianity is far more popular than the fully devoted variety.

Both Jason and Governor Pilate are sophisticated cynics. They know about Jesus and seem aware of his supreme leadership, but what other people demand overwhelms them. They doubt the value of true faith and can't stand up to the pressure of irresistible public opinion. "After all, who really knows what true truth is?" says Pilate (John 18:37–38, author's paraphrase). Jason says he merely "gets on the good side of the way things work." But what if Jesus is the human form of God, and humans ultimately account to him? Wouldn't that mean Jason and Pilate are making the biggest blunder of all?

Admitting to the dangerous shortsightedness of this cultural conformity, a thoughtful person might be ready for a turnaround choice to follow Jesus.

EIGHT

AT ODDS WITH GOD

As Jesus preaches and teaches, those most troubled by him usually belong to the top social class, where the same people fill both political and religious leadership roles. The Romans rule, but they incorporate local authorities into their collaborative occupational government. The second layer of government is comprised of religious groups—Pharisees, Sadducees, and the Sanhedrin—along with temple lawyers and the chief priest and his family. With few exceptions, they hate Jesus. They plot to kill him and eventually will succeed.

It could be leaders perceive his identity as a threat because they are so focused on protecting their own kingdoms. I've encapsulated an observation about human behavior into an axiom which says, "the bigger the stolen personal kingdom, the more ferocious the animosity toward the original owner." Jesus tells a convicting story, the Parable of the Tenants, about this sort of behavior:

Listen to another parable: There was a landowner who planted a vineyard. He put a wall around it, dug a winepress in it and built a watchtower. Then he rented the vineyard to some farmers and moved to another place. When the harvest time approached, he sent his servants to the tenants to collect his fruit.

The tenants seized his servants; they beat one, killed another, and stoned a third. Then he sent other servants to them, more than the first time, and the tenants treated them the same way. Last of all, he sent his son to them. "They will respect my son," he said.

But when the tenants saw the son, they said to each other, "This is the heir. Come, let's kill him and take his inheritance." So they took him and threw him out of the vineyard and killed him.

Therefore, when the owner of the vineyard comes, what will he do to those tenants? (Matt. 21:33–40)

His listeners blurt out the obvious, "He will bring those wretches to a wretched end" (v. 41). Then, incredibly, they begin to look for a way to arrest him because they understand he was talking about them!

So it's surprising that after Jesus's death and ascension to heaven, one of the most vicious enemies of the left-behind followers of Jesus eventually gives up his vendetta and pledges allegiance to Jesus.

An enemy of Jesus changes his mind.

Saul of Tarsus revels in a reputation for zealous pursuit of the Jewish Law with all its added refinements. In a letter he later sends to the church in Philippi, he lists his performance based on his credentials as a religious leader. He writes: "If someone else thinks they have reasons to put confidence in the flesh, I have more: circumcised on the eighth day, of the people of Israel, of the tribe of Benjamin, a Hebrew of the Hebrews; in regard to the law, a Pharisee; as for zeal, persecuting the church; as for righteousness based on the law, faultless" (Phil. 3:4–6).

Saul ranks among the elite religious influencers of his time. He jumps through all the social, cultural, and religious hoops and instinctively classifies Jesus as an archenemy. No one works more relentlessly to stamp out supporters of what was being called the Way. By killing followers of Jesus, Saul thinks he serves God and keeps Judaism pure. But then he meets the risen Lord face-to-face (Acts 9:1–19).

Full of rage and violent intent on the road to Damascus, Saul carries a legal permit to persecute, imprison, and kill those who believe Jesus is Messiah. His journey is interrupted in the middle of the day, as a light far brighter than the sun flattens him and his traveling companions.

A voice speaks from behind the stunning brightness: "Saul, Saul, why do you persecute me?" (v. 4).

Most likely, Saul pauses after that question. He is a brilliant man. His mind makes a fast calculation: *This is no man-made situation. No human could contrive such a light or speak from the sky. This must be God. But God is on my side! I am serving God with utmost zeal and the best of intentions. What could possibly make God think I would ever persecute him?*

Saul finally stammers, "Who are you, Lord?" And the answer shocks him more than he ever expected.

The voice answers, "I am Jesus, whom you are persecuting. Now get up and go into the city, and you will be told what you must do" (vv. 5–6). At that moment Saul is face-to-face with the realization he is terribly wrong. He's been fighting God while thinking he belongs on God's side. The trauma hits so hard, he can't see or eat. A physical blindness replaces his mental and spiritual blindness.

Saul's conversion is a confrontation, not an invitation.

The supreme authority in the universe has demonstrated his identity with unmistakable power and clarity. The Lord of All now allows Saul to sit in darkness for three days, pondering the arrogance behind his enormous blunder.

Then Jesus sends a man named Ananias to Saul, with orders to lay hands on him; Saul's sight will be restored and he will be filled with the Holy Spirit. When Ananias objects that Saul is dangerous, Jesus says he's chosen Saul as an instrument to carry his name before Gentiles and kings, as well as the children of Israel. Jesus assures Ananias that Saul will suffer much for spreading the gospel.

Ananias obeys, heals Saul's eyes, and immediately "something like scales" fall from them. Then Ananias baptizes Saul and feeds him (vv. 8–19).

Is Saul's conversion an exception to the norm of entering the kingdom through the free-will choices of repentance and faith? Some people believe this is a clear-cut case of "irresistible grace," or salvation through God's choice rather than ours. But there is more to the story.

Years later Paul (his new name after his encounter with Jesus) converses with King Agrippa and describes his conversion experience. He recalls what Jesus told him: "'I will rescue you from your own people and from the Gentiles. I am sending you to them to open their eyes and turn them from darkness to light, and from the power of Satan to God, so that they may receive forgiveness of sins and a place among those who are sanctified by faith in me.' So then, King Agrippa," he continues, "I was not disobedient to the vision from heaven. First to those in Damascus, then to those in Jerusalem and in all Judea, and then to the Gentiles, I preached that they should repent and turn to God and demonstrate their repentance by their deeds" (Acts 26:17–20).

Paul understands how to become a Christian. This involves repentance, a change of mind and heart about who leads in a person's life. He understands surrender to Jesus as Lord, not merely salvation through head knowledge. He experienced this. Paul's turnaround response, "Who are you, Lord?" that momentous day on the road to Damascus changed his life.

The Religious Zealot: *Saul*
Acts 9:1–19

Kingdom of Self
• Self-righteous
• Sure he was right
• Willing to persecute and kill

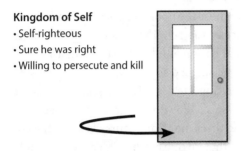

Kingdom of God
• Lived for God's purposes
• Became an apostle
• Served the cause of spreading the gospel

• Asked, "Who are you, Lord?"
• Admitted he was wrong
• Obeyed God
• Served God
• Forgiven by grace through faith

Smart people can have difficulty repenting.

One of the most intelligent people I've met was also extremely religious. Years ago he asked if I would teach a women's Bible study with him. For over a year he'd taught about one hundred women at a large restaurant in town.

I said I would love to talk about it and we began to meet. He immediately impressed me with his knowledge about church and world history. He'd earned two PhDs from a prestigious university, and was currently working on a third graduate degree. He was brilliant and ambitious.

He also held an influential position in his church: superintendent of education over one of the largest parochial school systems in the country. He shepherded 25,000 students from kindergarten through college. He was popular, well connected, and politically shrewd. I felt in awe of him, surprised he would ask a leader from a different faith tradition to partner with him. While meeting weekly for study, discussion, and planning, we became friends. At least it seemed that way to me.

For that year's study he chose the book of Ephesians, with much significant truth to process. My religious friend offered many insights into the historical background of the book that I didn't know. At the same time, he seemed to be learning how to listen for God's voice in interpreting the text. Then I sensed a change when we reached this passage: "For it is by grace you have been saved, through faith—and this is not from yourselves, it is the gift of God—not by works, so that no one can boast. For we are God's handiwork, created in Christ Jesus to do good works, which God prepared in advance for us to do" (Eph. 2:8–10).

After I explained what I thought the passage said about salvation, I asked for his interpretation. He read it out loud and then got a far-off look in his eyes. Finally he mumbled, "Justification by faith was a Protestant heresy that caused untold damage."

I gently asked, "But what does Scripture say? How do you understand its plain meaning?"

He did not answer.

Clearly, our study would progress no further that day, so I suggested he close our time in prayer. Then he said he resented me attempting to embarrass him. By this time, he clearly felt upset. This shocked me.

"Jan," he said, "I have never been able to pray without a written prayer in front of me and I suspect you know that. I just don't have the kind of relationship with Jesus that you seem to have. In fact, that's one of the reasons I asked you to teach this Bible study with me. I wanted some excitement and life-changing dynamic in the lessons, not just scholarship. I regret asking you now."

Stunned, I gently asked, "Do you want to pray naturally out of a close relationship with Jesus?" He remained silent for a long time. Then his eyes met mine and he said, "Is this where you make the pitch about being born again?"

It violated our relationship for him to say that. He realized this hurt me, but instead of apologizing, he got openly angry and continued on, as if what he imagined I was doing was actually taking place. "You evangelicals are so predictable. You think everyone else is inferior to you spiritually if they haven't come to faith by following your trite formula."

I began to tear up, confused and speechless. He stood up and left the room. I knew if he didn't apologize, our partnership would end. I felt blindsided by a latent animosity I never sensed in our previous meetings. In short, I'd never seen this coming.

The next day he sent me a note, canceling the Bible study because of "a full schedule." I attempted to meet with him again, but with no success. He cut off our relationship.

What was that?

As I reviewed our last encounter word by word, I eventually reached some conclusions. My intellectually religious friend covered up a personal kingdom-building pattern that left him deeply empty, restless, and angry. After all the studying and achievement, after all the ladder climbing, after all the degrees, titles, and rank in the religious arena, his heart remained distant and closed toward God.

As an expert, teacher, and religious authority, he gained a reputation as a promising and effective church leader. But his profession did not foster a genuine relationship with the God he represented. When a burst of spiritual insight hit him while we studied Ephesians, he recognized it as light and life. Then as he weighed the probable cost of losing his position in the hierarchy of his church, he backed away.

Unlike Paul, whom my friend resembled, he did not respond toward the Lord. He turned away from personally following Jesus and rejected me as a secondary reaction. By turning away from me, he acted out his primary choice of refusing Christ as Lord and Savior. The risk of losing his carefully constructed personal kingdom threatened him too much.

Since then, I've encountered this rejection many times. People who refuse to follow Jesus usually cannot stand those who do. No matter how kind and courteous Christ's followers try to be, rebellious people often spill anger on them.

When confronted by the living God, the human heart either surrenders or develops a self-serving hostility, sometimes carefully camouflaged. This is terribly unfair. In a world of injustice, resisting and rejecting God's love through Jesus proves the greatest injustice of all. God deserves to be our leader. He uniquely possesses a capacity for love without limits. He doesn't deserve mocking and scorn. He doesn't deserve cheap shots and angry jabs. He deserves trust and respect. But nothing seems more common on this rebelling planet than the God-hatred of a road-to-Damascus experience gone wrong.

God always speaks. He confronts proud and arrogant people about their theft of his throne. God reveals himself through Jesus, the Lord of all and Savior of all. Some smart people repent and give up their lifelong preoccupation with a self-designed god who approves of their self-controlled life. Others, equally intelligent but terminally stubborn, shake off the light of God's revelation of himself and his interrupting voice. Those who turn toward God alter their personal history and lose their restlessness. Those who turn away repeat their history. Each of us is ultimately defined by which way we turn.

God created us and carefully planned the arrival of Jesus with his mission to live and die among us. But he isn't done yet. He planned that I would hear his amazing message about his accessible kingdom. He planned for you to hear it, too.

PART TWO

COMING TO THE END OF RESTLESSNESS

"You will seek me and find me when you seek me with all your heart. I will be found by you," declares the LORD.

Jeremiah 29:13–14

In the end, coming to faith remains for all a sense of homecoming, of picking up the threads of a lost life, of responding to a bell that had long been ringing, of taking a place at a table that had long been vacant.

Malcolm Muggeridge (1903–1990),
journalist, author, broadcaster, Christian apologist

Creatures are not born with desires unless satisfaction for those desires exists. A baby feels hunger: well, there is such a thing as food. A duckling wants to swim: well, there is such a thing as water. People feel sexual desire: well, there is such a thing as sex. If I find in myself a desire which no experience in this world can satisfy, the most probable explanation is that I was made for another world. If none of my earthly pleasures satisfy it that does not prove the universe is a fraud. Probably earthly pleasures were never meant to satisfy it, but only arouse it, to suggest the real thing.

C. S. Lewis, Mere Christianity

NINE

CURIOUS ABOUT GOD

I know something about religious leadership. For most of my adult life, serving church congregations gave me exhilarating joy. Three churches, over a period of forty-five years, trusted me with pastoral leadership. I wouldn't trade this experience for anything. At the same time I admit that powerful temptations, unique to ministers, obstruct the ministry career path.

The most common temptations appear at the ego level. When a group of people say you are their model, when they give you honor and respect, it can easily go to your head. I fought the urge to consider myself spiritually special and superior. But I knew the reality of my inner world behind the public performance. I didn't want to pretend to be godlier than I actually was, or to preach beyond my experience, but at times I did.

Many people assume religious people, especially leaders, are different from the rest of us. The clergy mystique blinds people, making them think church leaders do not face the common temptation to build and maintain their own kingdoms. Unfortunately, religious trappings, pageantry, rituals, and traditions provide an unexpected place to hide selfishness.

Some feel shocked or, more likely, delighted when religious celebrities fall on their faces. Their scandalous behavior seems worse than others who do the same things. Aren't the religious supposed to be better? More moral and ethical, more humble and selfless, than ordinary people? We call them hypocrites, and that might be true. But when we think fairly about it, using any accurate standard, we're all hypocrites. We don't live up to our beliefs and values. It's just more obvious with religious professionals.

Religion can twist into a maze of kingdoms. The confusing varieties of religious kingdoms bear witness that "doing your own thing for God" attracts multitudes of participants. Egoism and power trips plague religious circles. Religious pride and arrogance exist in all faiths, denominations, sects, and cults.

A universal self-centeredness and need for control can thrive in every brand of religion. Religious groups tend to treat symptoms instead of causes, sanctioning and sanitizing the disease they could eradicate. They build pride, prejudice, and self-righteousness instead of peaceful communities of love and humility. Regrettably, many of our religious kingdoms try to impress God with what they can do rather than letting God impress us with who he is and what he does.

We stir up trouble whenever we tell the truth.

According to Scripture, Jesus stirs up trouble with the religious people in his native culture. Devout Jews base their religious system on God's message in the Old Testament. Because God spoke clearly to ancient Jewish leaders, the religious leaders Jesus met enjoyed enormous privileges and advantages compared to others. But for the most part these leaders had turned religion into a rigid system of complex rules and regulations only a trained expert could understand and interpret, let alone master. In their circle it is politically incorrect to befriend Jesus. The religious class not only rejects him out of hand, they act like attack dogs toward him.

Because of this religious and political climate, Nicodemus visits Jesus at night. A top authority on Old Testament Scriptures, he is a legitimate big shot among his people. He cannot afford for anyone to know about his serious talks with Jesus. The gospel of John records his clandestine conversation with the controversial teacher from Galilee (3:1–15).

Nicodemus, a Pharisee, belongs to the Sanhedrin, the Jewish ruling council. He prides himself as the number-one communicator in the country. Jesus refers to him as "Israel's teacher" (v. 10). Clearly, a religious celebrity. With a carefully constructed image, he exercises caution and anonymity when conversing with Jesus.

Knowing Nicodemus is on a serious mission, Jesus doesn't mince words: "Very truly I tell you, no one can see the kingdom of God unless they are born again" (v. 3). That must sound strange to Nicodemus. Today "born again" is a common term in evangelical Christian circles. Even outside of these circles, many people at least hear it somewhere in the media culture. But in Nicodemus's time, it probably made no sense. He naturally took Jesus's statement at face value.

Nicodemus asks, "How can anyone be born who has already been born and grown up? You can't re-enter your mother's womb and be born again" (v. 4 MSG). Nicodemus isn't being sarcastic. He wants to figure out what Jesus means.

He doesn't wait long. Jesus answers, "Don't be so surprised when I tell you that you have to be 'born from above'—out of this world, so to speak. You know well enough how the wind blows this way and that. You hear it rustling through the trees, but you have no idea where it comes from or where it's headed next. That's the way it is with everyone 'born from above' by the wind of God, the Spirit of God" (vv. 7–8 MSG).

Talk about metaphysical language! Does Jesus deliberately mess with this man's mind? Nicodemus carefully follows a religious system, spelled out in a list of rules and a rigid prescription for every conceivable life situation. Teachers like Nicodemus encourage their students to focus and work hard. Now Jesus turns performance-based spirituality upside down. Likening kingdom entrance to birth makes it something a human cannot do. It requires a miracle.

We can appear pious even while still self-enthroned.

Nicodemus arrives asking how to enter the kingdom of God. So something must be missing from his world of rules. Jesus insists Nicodemus brings nothing to the table, nothing to commend him to God, nothing to pry open the door to heaven. Such a counter-intuitive idea probably shocks this religious seeker.

From a human perspective, Nicodemus perfectly positions himself at the head of the line. He expects not only automatic entrance but outright exoneration in God's kingdom. It shatters Nicodemus to learn he needs to start back at the metaphorical womb. Basically Jesus says, "Nicodemus, the ladder you're climbing so diligently is leaning against the wrong wall. In fact, you don't even need a ladder; you need me. I'm the Door. I'm the Way in. I'm the one essential requirement. All your painstaking attention to religious rituals and regulations will get you nowhere. You have a problem. All of your religious achievements fortify your own kingdom. You control everything even though you talk about God a lot. In your human obsession with doing 'God's thing' your way, you appear pious while remaining firmly seated on the throne of your heart."

Nicodemus fools other people, and most of the time himself, but he can't get his kingdom issues past Jesus. Nor can he hide his restlessness. His heart tumbles to its emotional basement with a thud. "What do you mean by this?" he plaintively asks (v. 9 MSG).

Jesus responds, "You're a respected teacher of Israel and you don't know these basics?" (v. 10 MSG).

By now the clandestine discussion passes into the early morning. Jesus teaches Nicodemus a crash course on the essentials of a born-again entrance into God's kingdom. First Jesus asserts himself as the expert. His is the valid testimony because he descended from heaven. Only he can clear up the fog rising from religious speculation.

Honoring Nicodemus's knowledge of the Old Testament, Jesus introduces his favorite title for himself: Son of Man. That unique name causes Nicodemus to remember the greatest recorded glimpse of heaven's throne room. The prophet Daniel sets the stage, amazed in God's presence: "As I was watching all this, 'Thrones were set in place and the Old One sat down. His robes were white as snow, his hair was white like wool. His throne was flaming with fire, its wheels blazing. A river of fire poured out of the throne. Thousands upon thousands served him, tens of thousands attended him. The courtroom was called to order, and the books were opened'" (Dan. 7:9–10 MSG).

What a magnificent vision! Undoubtedly, from this passage Nicodemus teaches Israel about the holiness, justice, and majesty of the eternal God. Without question, he knows what happens next: "I saw a human form, a son of man, arriving in a whirl of clouds. He came to The Old One and was presented to him. He was given power to rule—all the glory of royalty. Everyone—race, color, and creed—had to serve him. His rule would be forever, never ending. His kingly rule would never be replaced" (vv. 13–14 MSG).

Nicodemus is undoubtedly thinking, *Oh my goodness! You're that Son of Man!* You can almost see the consternation on his face as he processes Jesus's identity. No wonder Nicodemus found it impossible to shake off the urge to talk with him.

There is an antidote to sin's snakebite.

What Jesus says next makes sense to this Pharisee. "In the same way that Moses lifted the serpent in the desert so people could have something to see and then believe, it is necessary for the Son of Man to be lifted up—and everyone who looks up to him, trusting and expectant, will gain a real life, eternal life" (John 3:14–15 MSG).

Jesus refers to an incident recorded in Numbers, the fourth book in the Jewish Torah (the first five books in the Hebrew Scriptures and the Old Testament). In the ancient story, the Jewish people grumble against God and their leader, Moses. After all God's faithful provision and miraculous meeting of their needs, the people's recurring, blatant ingratitude moves the Lord to serious discipline.

The account says, "God sent poisonous snakes among the people; they bit them and many in Israel died" (Num. 21:6 MSG). Immediately the people changed their tune and confessed their defiance. They begged Moses to take away the snakes. Moses prayed, and God answered with these instructions: "'Make a snake and put it on a flagpole: Whoever is bitten and looks at it will live.' So Moses made a snake of fiery copper and put it on top of a flagpole. Anyone bitten by a snake who then looked at the copper snake lived" (vv. 8–9 MSG).

By this time Nicodemus's theological world with its neat categories disintegrates into shambles. Jesus's message makes sense.

Jesus connects the dots in the conversation. "Nicodemus," Jesus insists, "you need me. I am as necessary to your entrance into God's kingdom as the bronze snake was indispensable to the bitten and dying Israelites of old. Believe in me; trust me as the only one who can give you eternal life, and a new birth into life in God's kingdom will be yours" (author's paraphrase).

These words overwhelm Nicodemus. The way into the kingdom is the King! His eternal realm is available and waits for him—but not through self-generated, self-assertive, self-exalting religious performance.

Placing the kingdom picture over Nicodemus's life recalls rich people whom Jesus encounters, wrapped in their titles and possessions. This man's religious accomplishments form impressive walls around his personal kingdom. However, Jesus only uses the born-again language with Nicodemus. The New Testament does not record anyone else hearing his message in this particular way.

The Ruling Council Member: *Nicodemus*
John 3:1-21

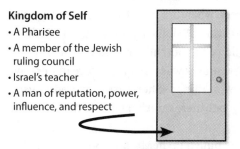

Kingdom of Self
- A Pharisee
- A member of the Jewish ruling council
- Israel's teacher
- A man of reputation, power, influence, and respect

Kingdom of God
Holy Spirit–generated eternal life now and forever

- Be born again without earning it
- Give up religious kingdom
- Believe Jesus, "the Son of Man," is the way into God's kingdom

Why wouldn't Jesus have used this terminology elsewhere? Because this man's specific kingdom issues need this approach. Jesus uses a carefully adjusted version of his good news with each individual. Yet he still focuses on surrendering the unique kingdom of self-in-control that each person, by human nature, inevitably builds for self-identification and false security.

According to historical record, Nicodemus becomes a follower of Jesus. After the crucifixion, he and Joseph of Arimathea, another convert from the ruling council, take the Lord's body down from the cross, prepare it for burial, and seal it in Joseph's tomb. Nicodemus no longer worries about what others think. When it counts, he stands by Jesus. The resurrection probably doesn't surprise him. He understands the Son of Man's identity. From this enlightened perspective, who or what could stop God's choice of a supreme leader?

What happens if we actually let God into our life?

A single, well-paid computer consultant and classical musician, Sherri turns thirty this year. She enjoys a rich, full life, and wouldn't trade it, except once in a while when she spends time with her friend Joan. Last week when the two friends walked around Green Lake, it happened again. A slight Washington drizzle didn't bother them as they followed a footpath around the lake.

Joan talked about how prayer was a strong fixture in her day.

"Do you pray about everything?" Sherri asked incredulously.

"No, not consciously, but there's not much that doesn't come up eventually."

Sherri protested as she pulled up her hood, "But don't you feel like you're just talking to yourself? How do you know God is even listening to you or cares what's going on in your mind or your life?"

Joan thought for a while, then responded, "The only way I can answer that is to tell you that God is real to me, Sherri. I used to think prayer was just wishful thinking for weak people, but I don't anymore. I feel close to God and I'm sure he listens when I talk to him. He answers me and I know he . . ." She grinned. "Well, he actually likes me and wants to help."

Sherri changed the subject and finished the walk by telling a humorous story from her childhood. But over the next few days, Sherri wished she'd asked more questions. She repeatedly wondered about opening up communication with God.

Sherri is closing the distance between her heart and God for the best of reasons. For a long time she's believed he exists; now she wants to know him. For Sherri, God is changing slowly from an idea-God to a knowable, lovable person-God.

On the other hand, deep inside, she's apprehensive. She's wondering: What will happen to me if I actually let God into my life? After all, this is God I'm dealing with. She'd like to be closer to him, but doesn't want to change. She feels uncomfortable moving from believing in God to giving him authority. She is intelligent and honest enough to know she should expect God to act like God.

We can always take the religion detour.

In the past, Sherri used religion to escape a divine takeover. A God she visits in church feels less disruptive than one who leads her life. The God of organized religion makes little impact on the real world of her day-to-day existence.

Most of us can identify with this sincere woman. We may be a religious professional like Nicodemus, or a spiritual sampler like Sherri. We may have accepted Jesus as Savior, but not yet given control of our life to him. This is a recipe for continuing restlessness. The kingdom message and its significance can stimulate us toward reexamining an understanding of what God actually desires from us. Some people get trapped in their own choices and start thinking about God. Others feel a growing hunger for God, like Nicodemus or Sherri.

More personally, do you sense God trying to get your attention? It may not be a sequence of disappointing or painful circumstances that stir your heart. It could just be a feeling that something's missing. You're inwardly restless and motivated to look for more. However you're drawn to God, don't push him away. Let curiosity lead to faith. Follow the example of Nicodemus. Look with a believing heart to the One who opens the door to God's kingdom. Bow and believe. Look and eternally live.

TEN

THIRSTY FOR GOD

Anyone who enrolls in Psychology 101 in college learns about Maslow's hierarchy of human needs. In the 1940s the psychologist Abraham Maslow developed a theory about these needs. He identified a person's basic needs as physiological, safety, love and belonging, esteem, and self-actualization. He illustrated these needs by placing the most basic ones, physiological, at the bottom of a pyramid. The other ones, in the order just listed, build progressively and depend upon one another. For example, it's difficult for someone to develop esteem if physiological needs aren't fulfilled. Maslow's hierarchy still offers insight to students today (see page 112).

Interestingly, many of Maslow's observations coincide with the Bible. The Creator of the human psyche comprehends our physical and psychological needs. But in addition to these necessities, he designed us with spiritual needs that few psychologists acknowledge. We need him! He created us to function best when we accept him as our loving leader. He is the "software," we are the "hardware." When we load him on our heart-drive, we function according to his original design. When we try to operate without him, we mess up.

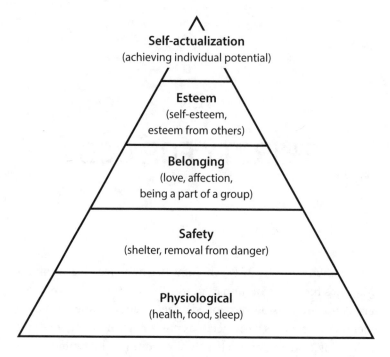

Trying but failing is a familiar experience.

A particular woman tries to fulfill her needs, but mostly fails. She is a Samaritan, carrying mixed blood: part Jewish and part Assyrian. The conquests of Sargon II and King Esarhaddon left their mark on Palestine in more than architecture and literature. The resulting half-breed people live as outcasts, shunned by the pure Hebrew population.

The Samaritan woman encounters Jesus at Jacob's well, near the town of Sychar (modern-day Askar). Tired from a journey, Jesus rests there while his disciples walk to town for something to eat. The woman arrives at the well around noon.

She shows up at the worst time for drawing water. The sun blazes down in full heat. Most people draw water in the morning or evening, in cooler temperatures. She probably deliberately avoids other women in the community. She knows what they think of her. She lives as an outcast within a community of outcasts. The conversation begins when Jesus asks her for a drink. With no container or rope to draw from the deep well, it makes sense to ask. But his request surprises her.

"You're a Jew. I am a Samaritan and besides that, I am a woman. So how can you even consider asking me for a drink, since you Jews don't associate with us Samaritans?" Clearly she realizes his predicament. He needs help to quench his physical thirst. Taking advantage of the opportunity, she vents her resentment toward the Jews and others.

Jesus answers her, "If you knew the generosity of God and who I am, you would be asking me for a drink, and I would give you fresh, living water."

Reading between the lines I hear her say, "Very funny, mister. You must think you are something special. You have no water, no means of getting water, and yet you act like you're some kind of invisible water supplier. Who do you think you are? Are you greater than our father Jacob, who dug this well and drank from it himself? Come on, get real!"

I think Jesus enjoys her spunk. Patiently he says, "Everyone who drinks this water will get thirsty again and again. Anyone who drinks the water I give will never thirst—not ever. The water I give will be an artesian spring within, gushing fountains of endless life."

Amused by Jesus, I hear her saying, "Okay, I'll call your bluff. Go ahead, give me this water of yours so I won't get thirsty and have to keep coming back out here to this old well."

Then abruptly, Jesus gets personal. "Go call your husband and then come back." He doesn't intend to embarrass the woman or make her feel guilty, but he uncovers her makeshift kingdom.

"I have no husband," she replies.

"You are certainly right about that," Jesus says. "The fact is you've had five husbands and the man you are living with now you haven't even bothered to marry. You spoke the truth there, sure enough."

"Wow," she sputters, struggling to recover from a stranger confronting her about the skeletons in her closet. "You must be some kind of a prophet! You'd have to be to know about my private life."

Trying to change the subject isn't going to work.

Now her mind races. *Where do I take this from here? I know! I'll change the subject. I'll bring up the topic no Jew can resist arguing about.*

"Since you're so knowledgeable, perhaps you can settle an issue that has long puzzled me. Our ancestors worshiped God at this mountain, but you Jews insist Jerusalem is the only place for worship, right? Help me out here. Which is it?"

Jesus deliberately accepts the change of subject and offers one of the most profound discussions of worship in the New Testament. He refuses to debate the matter of which geographic place is best. Then he says, "Believe me, woman, the time is coming when you Samaritans will worship the Father neither here at this mountain nor there in Jerusalem. You worship guessing in the dark; we Jews worship in the clear light of day. God's way of salvation is made available through the Jews. But the time is coming—it has, in fact, come—when what you're called will not matter and where you go to worship will not matter.

"It's who you are and the way you live that count before God. Your worship must engage your spirit in the pursuit of truth. That's the kind of people the Father is looking for: those who are simply and honestly themselves before him in their worship. God is sheer being itself—Spirit. Those who worship him must do it out of their very being, their spirits, their true selves, in adoration."

This overwhelms her again. The stranger keeps her off balance.

"Look," she says, "I don't know about that. I do know the Messiah is coming. When he arrives, we'll get the whole story."

And now the battering ram slams into the door of her heart. Jesus declares, "I'm the man you're talking about!"

She's been trying to meet her needs, fulfilling her heart's longings in masculine wells that don't satisfy her quest for significance, security, and self-worth. Now she faces the God-man, the Messiah, the leader of God's kingdom. This man offers the soul satisfaction she's searched for all her life.

In an instant everything falls into place for the Samaritan woman. First, the opening discussion of water that permanently satisfies thirst. Second, Jesus knows about the succession of men in her life. Third, he is the Messiah. With these realizations, she rushes into town to proclaim her discovery of the Christ of God. Just as Jesus predicts, she becomes a soul-satisfying source of Living Water, pouring into the lives of many. (See John 4:1–30; adapted from the MSG.)

Placing a kingdom grid over the Samaritan woman's life looks like this:

The Samaritan Woman
John 4:1–26

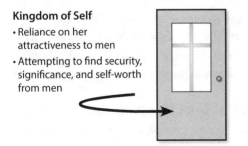

Kingdom of Self
- Reliance on her attractiveness to men
- Attempting to find security, significance, and self-worth from men

Kingdom of God
- Eternal life
- A wellspring that bubbled up in her and attracted others
- The Holy Spirit (John 7:37–39)

- "Where can you get living water?"
- Stop trying to satisfy your soul's thirst through your own devices

Later, Jesus clarifies the metaphor of a thirsty heart swelling into a life-giving stream. Jesus tells a huge crowd gathered to observe the Jewish Feast of Tabernacles, "'If anyone thirsts, let him come to me and drink. Rivers of living water will brim and spill out of the depths of anyone who believes in me this way, just as the Scripture says.' (He said this in regard to the Spirit, whom those who believed in him were about to receive)" (John 7:37–39 MSG).

When God's Spirit takes up residence in a person, life can flow with fulfillment and satisfaction.

He is the only love that never fails.

Like the woman at the well—and as shown in Maslow's hierarchy—we need love and belonging. However, if we build kingdoms through love relationships, expecting them to fill the hollow spaces in the heart, they will disappoint or fail us. Many people make the erroneous assumption that if they just find the right man or woman, they will live happily ever after.

Even more trouble breaks out when they never stop shopping. They discard people with imperfections because they're annoyed. They refuse to change their own grating or addictive habits. They grow bored by the everyday aspects of relationships. Partners who age become expendable. Younger, more attractive options entice. They confuse physical intimacy with love, seeking many sex partners. They engage in multiple relationships before and after marriage, patching up crumbling love kingdoms.

Jesus understands this quest for love. We all need love. Scripture tells several stories of Jesus's compassion for people desperately searching for love, especially those who choose immoral paths to find it. He forgives and points them to the true source of belonging.

*Crashing the party with heartfelt gratitude
can be misunderstood.*

Simon the Pharisee, a scholarly religious leader, invites Jesus to a dinner party. The guests no sooner settle comfortably around the table, than a known streetwalker crashes the gathering. The woman carries her savings account in her hands. In her culture, people invest in expensive perfume that can be resold when they need extra money. Holding an alabaster jar of precious perfume, she walks directly to Jesus. She weeps so profusely her tears wet his feet. With her flowing hair she wipes his feet and kisses them.

Then she lavishes her treasured perfume on the Lord's feet, but it's not a sensual act. It's sacred. Love and gratitude pour from her heart. Something holy takes place; a desperately needy soul worships the Messiah.

Simon the Pharisee watches what for him was a shocking sight. *If this man were a legitimate prophet, he would have the discernment to know who is touching him. This extravagant display of adoration is ludicrous because of the kind of woman doing it. What a joke! Apparently, everybody but Jesus knows she's a notorious sinner.*

Jesus reads Simon's mind from across the room. He says, "Simon, I have something to tell you."

Guests can almost hear the condescension dripping from the Pharisee's reply. "Tell me, Teacher."

Jesus then tells a story. "Two men were in debt to a banker. One owed five hundred silver pieces, the other fifty. Neither of them could pay up, and so the banker canceled both debts. Which of the two would be more grateful?"

What can Simon say? "Well, I suppose the one who had the bigger debt canceled would show more gratitude."

"That's right." Jesus nods. Then he turns and faces the woman while still talking to the Pharisee.

"Do you see this woman? I came to your home; you provided no water for my feet, but she rained tears on my feet and dried them with her hair. You gave me no greeting, but from the time I arrived she hasn't quit kissing my feet. You provided nothing for freshening up, but she has soothed my feet with perfume. Impressive, isn't it? She was forgiven many, many sins, and so she is very, very grateful. If the forgiveness is minimal, the gratitude is minimal."

To the woman he says, "I forgive your sins."

The guests could hear a pin drop in the high drama of the moment. Then they whisper among themselves about the blasphemous arrogance of Jesus, daring to suggest he could forgive sins. Jesus ignores them and says to the woman, "Your faith has saved you. Go in peace." (See Luke 7:36–50; adapted from the MSG.)

God's acceptance and forgiveness provoke intense response.

Clearly this event signifies not just the woman's salvation from her life of commercialized sex, but her entrance into the kingdom of God. But is this what it takes to gain his favor—fawning and crawling in abject humility? Is this how true faith acts?

Adding in the ingredients of sin and shame, and her certainty of Jesus's true identity, a different reading of her behavior emerges. She acts like someone who believes Jesus is God and his forgiveness is her only hope. Not all will identify with this story but many will, especially those who live with shame, rejection, and self-loathing because of destructive personal choices.

Before the woman poured out her treasure, she probably had followed Jesus for weeks, hiding in the crowds, carefully watching. She listened closely, growing convinced Jesus and his heavenly Father are one. She sensed he would be loving and approachable, in spite of how other people see her and how she berates herself.

In visual terms, the woman's journey looks like this:

The Woman with the Worst of Reputations
Luke 7:36–50

Kingdom of Self
- Doing whatever it took to survive without regard for God's ownership or leadership
- Sinning herself into a life of guilt, shame, and rejection

Kingdom of God
- "Your sins are forgiven. Your faith has saved you; go in peace."
- Jesus saw in her heart the love of one whose huge debt had been canceled

- Her attitude of humility
- Her gratitude lavishly poured out
- Her tears of shame and remorse

Often our needs bring us to God. Maslow was right about how powerful those needs can be. God is right about our ultimate need for a love relationship with him. Our attempts to meet needs in our own way can trap us behind kingdom walls of guilt and shame. Building a kingdom might not be our intention; we just wanted to love and be loved. But we leave God out.

According to Jesus, repentant faith is the best way to meet our need for love.

He provided for our total and complete forgiveness at great cost to himself. He is willing to work with us while picking up the pieces of our lives. He eagerly wants to meet our needs and lead us in a process of reconstruction in his kingdom. Our part necessitates leaving our old familiar kingdom of failed loves and trusting his offer of forgiveness and restored relationship. Stepping through the door to peace by making a faith choice, we embark on a life of joy, peace, and love in his kingdom.

ELEVEN

QUESTIONING GOD

Critics describe the Christian belief system as non-intellectual or even anti-intellectual. But could the reverse actually be true? What if genuine, thinking faith does not demand that all questions need answers? What if we leave room for mystery or unknowns? The existence of doubt does not mean suspending belief. Skepticism does not automatically invalidate hypotheses or theories. If it did, we'd need to declare scientific research invalid and a time waster. Scientists know skepticism can lead to exploration and deeper insights, from doubt to plausible reasons to believe.

For many, intellectual engagement, scientific fact, and experiential truth are essential to faith. But a refusal to believe usually is not about an inability to believe.

Skepticism monopolizes a position of power. First, the person who claims unbelief or suspended belief avoids commitment. Unbelief demands no allegiance except to the self. A life built on questions rather than answers masquerades as intellectual high ground. However, it's usually a convenient way to float above the demands of a belief system, to evade responsibility. Second, nothing to believe means nothing to defend, no mental turf to protect. Cleverly, this position pours energy into attacking others, but people with belief systems can't counter nothingness. Supposedly, nonbelievers live free from explanation.

When Jesus walked the earth, doubters surrounded him with a well-designed strategy for his destruction. Enemies and critics bombarded him with carefully constructed skepticism. They fervently disputed his claims to truth. At every turn, they challenged his teaching and actions, especially his miracles. Supernatural acts developed faith in some and unbelief in others.

The tension in the four gospels of the New Testament burgeoned from a relentless campaign of hostility and misinformation. When attackers ran out of coherent arguments, they accused Jesus of joining the devil's league (Matt. 12:24–28). This kind of doubt strategy emerges from God's hardened opponents. But another type of doubter exists, the honest doubters. By "honest doubt" I refer to sincere people who don't possess adequate information or those for whom some things don't make sense. These doubters puzzle and search for missing parts. When honest doubters find new pieces that fit into the spiritual puzzle, they easily discard skeptical questions.

Jesus welcomes honest doubters.

Thomas the disciple doesn't fit the profile of a strategic skeptic. Although he belongs to Jesus's inner circle of friends and followers, he doesn't classify as a blind loyalist either. Historically, Thomas gains the reputation of *doubter* because he won't buy into the grief hysteria after Jesus's crucifixion. But for the most part, Thomas harbors honest doubts. He hears the claims of eyewitnesses to the resurrection. Their stories sound like the irrational things shocked people say during overwhelming grief and loss. Their accounts don't seem plausible.

Understandably, Thomas probably protects his heart from further disappointment and deeper despair. Like the other disciples, Jesus's death shatters his hopes for the kingdom of heaven established on earth. The crucifixion devastates and disillusions this sensitive man. He closes his mind to reconstructing broken dreams.

In the presence of disciples who claim Jesus rose from the dead, Thomas says aloud, "Unless I see the nail marks in his hands and put my fingers where the nails were, and put my hand into his side, I will not believe" (John 20:25). Honest doubt demanding proof. Not a hardness of heart speaking, but rather, the searing pain of deep disappointment. "If he's alive, where is he?"

God approaches honest doubters with extreme patience. In this case, Jesus gives Thomas individual attention. After eight excruciating days in the agony and limbo of skepticism, Thomas needs it. Jesus appears to him in the presence of other close followers and says, "Put your finger here; see my hands. Reach out your hand and put it into my side. Stop doubting and believe" (v. 27).

Thomas does not keep his suspended belief intact. Face-to-face with Jesus, he bows to the observable facts. Not a figment of imagination, the risen Lord is touchable and Thomas examines wounds on the resurrected body. In a whiplash of realization, he then blurts out, "My Lord and my God!" (v. 28). His protective shell cracks and faith floods back into his heart. But his personal conversation with Jesus continues. The Lord tells Thomas, probably with great tenderness, "Because you have seen me, you have believed; blessed are those who have not seen and yet have believed" (v. 29).

Faith is not without supporting evidence.

Does Jesus's remark seem unreasonable or harsh? Does his comment indicate a hierarchy of belief? Does this mean faith with evidence is not as valuable as faith without evidence? It sounds like a "leap of faith" really matters. The Bible clearly states that "faith is confidence in what we hope for and assurance about what we do not see" (Heb. 11:1). Evidence supports faith, but it may not always be empirical evidence, at least not immediately discernible evidence.

God's activity in our lives and in our world is self-evident if we choose to remember, recognize, and credit it. What has God already done? That's the key question.

Jesus expects his disciples to remember the three years they traveled together. Jesus reproves Thomas because he forgets the evidence already in front of his eyes. Thomas has seen Jesus prove his authority over demons, disease, and death. He watched the Master calm a raging storm. He witnessed the blind receiving sight, the lame walking, and lepers being healed. He ate food from a boy's modest lunch, multiplied by Jesus to feed five thousand men plus their women and children. In other words, Thomas has collected a ton of personal knowledge about Jesus's divine credentials.

On top of that, he stood within earshot when Jesus announced his upcoming death and resurrection. These events don't exactly spring on the disciples with no warning. Yet when tested with a severe loss of expectation, Thomas forgets his Lord's identity. That leads me to suspect Thomas's hesitation is not an isolated incident.

In my experience, skepticism can be a response to things we don't understand. It often starts early in adolescence as a need to question everything, and then grows into a prove-it-to-me attitude in adulthood. Doubt becomes a fallback reaction to protect ourselves from disappointment or mistakes in judgment. Actually, doubt can protect us from those negatives, but it also blinds us to reality.

Doubt compares to a pair of dark sunglasses. They filter the real world and change color perceptions into shades of black, grey, and white. In other words, these metaphorical glasses set up a "way of seeing," altered by the lenses of doubts and questions. Likewise, a cynical mind-set hardens into the habitual way we chose to do life. Once established, we find it difficult to change thinking patterns. We often invest great effort into sustaining unbelief. Anything challenging our cherished doubts—even with clear and logical answers—requires serious resistance. If we are bent toward unbelief, this description of skepticism may hit near the mark.

The Doubter: Thomas
John 20:24–31

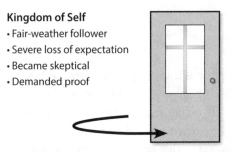

Kingdom of Self
- Fair-weather follower
- Severe loss of expectation
- Became skeptical
- Demanded proof

Kingdom of God
Became a lifetime
ambassador for Jesus

- "My Lord and my God!"
- Let go of his doubts

Jesus graciously fulfills Thomas's demand for empirical evidence because this disciple opens his heart to belief. In seconds, Thomas rockets from cynicism to worship. In another biblical report (Luke 24:33–43), other disciples experienced disbelief also, even after Jesus displays his hands and feet. At first blush, the next phrase in the account doesn't fit; the writer says these doubters "still did not believe it because of joy and amazement." It obviously was one of those times where you had to have been there in order to understand. But my point is, Thomas was not alone. All the disciples had their faith revived. All of them struggled with doubt.

Like them, we might feel frozen when a new experience or discovery challenges what we think. Can we intellectually assimilate new facts over a lifetime? In my experience, Jesus always welcomes honest doubters. He reveals himself and reasons with us while we process his truth. He tenderly reminds us what we already know but sometimes forget.

Many times Jesus has met me in my fog of incomplete and inadequate perceptions. I cried out in intellectual confusion and frustration, and he answered with gentleness and patience, providing the help I needed. He will do the same for anyone not at war with him.

Doubt can be a weapon.

Cindy enjoys her exceptional thinking ability. She has soared off the charts of every intelligence-testing tool she's taken. Her intelligence anchors her self-image and confidence. Somewhere along the line, though, she turned toward spiritual skepticism, making it her fallback position. This amazing woman views life as a chess game. She's usually several moves ahead of everyone else. And she's at war with God.

Cindy grew up in the Far East bouncing between a missionary home and a boarding school. She knows the Bible and how to navigate the conservative Christian culture. When we first met, she easily passed as an "insider," a believer in a community of faith. Unfortunately, it took a while to realize that Cindy mastered the appearance of devout faith to manipulate people. I gradually became aware that she was a brilliant actress, but definitely not a Christian. What tipped me off? Cindy exhibited absolutely no fear of God. She did not care what God thought of her behavior. She deceived and sabotaged others at an astonishing level.

In one month, Cindy destroyed the leadership of the church she and her now-retired parents attended. She launched a campaign of slander and malicious rumor manufactured from thin air. Destroying the reputations of good people—those she had lived and worked with for years—was incredibly easy for her. In fact, she enjoyed it. I consoled her parents the day she taunted them with her unbelief. She felt no remorse about her deceptions.

When Cindy's dad asked how she could justify the destructive accusations and events she set in motion, she replied, "You people deserve to be taken advantage of. Your belief in God makes you vulnerable to cynics like me. I've done you a favor by showing you in painfully graphic terms that God doesn't exist. He didn't protect you from my deceptions and he didn't reveal to you the enemy in your midst. Why can't you admit you're deluded and misguided in your so-called faith?" She confidently believed her power to deceive and destroy proved God did not exist.

Cindy's audacity stunned me and broke her parents' hearts. We tried to give her every benefit of the doubt, thinking she might be acting out of childhood abuse or perhaps another tragedy suffered while her parents served as missionaries. She laughed at our attempt to offer mercy and grace. She thought our suggestion she might need counseling was hilarious.

She complained, "Why can't you just get it through your heads that I am the way I am and I do the things I do because I hate the very concept of God? People who believe in him are out of touch with reality and pathetically behind the times. If we are going to achieve the next level in our evolutionary development as a species, belief in God has got to be eradicated. And by the way, my unbelief started and developed in my university training. The smartest people I've ever met helped me dismantle my faith and I'm grateful they did."

I asked Cindy why she had infiltrated our church and worked hard to win our trust. Why couldn't she just leave us alone? Her answer took my breath away. She announced. "I am at war with religion, the Bible, the church, and everything you people stand for. I see religion as the most destructive element in our world today, and I am determined to tear down as much of it as I can."

Sadly, Cindy is not alone in her war with God. Millions agree with her, although they might not approve of her methods. In recent years several best-selling authors unabashedly designed their books as faith-crushers. As avowed atheists and professional unbelievers, they want to save humanity from the "evils" of faith in God. There's no doubt about it, aggressive unbelief has become the accepted educational philosophy of the Western world.

Is high IQ a deterrent to faith?

So is it true that the brightest people don't believe in God, or suspend belief as their capacity to reason increases? Is low IQ a necessary requirement for belief in God? People like Cindy would say yes. But they don't know much about history. These, and many more, intelligent people were Christians:

- Blaise Pascal, famous French mathematician
- Isaac Newton, world renowned mathematician and physicist
- Galileo Galilei, Italian physicist
- Johannes Kepler, German astronomer
- Samuel Morse, inventor of Morse Code
- The Wright brothers, modern aviation pioneers

Many of the pioneers of science expressed deep faith in God. Many of the people who started schools and universities were Christians. Many of the people who established hospitals and made breakthrough discoveries in modern medicine were Christians. Christians discovered the wonders of electricity, and invented the light bulb, the telegraph, and other innovations that created the modern world. It's easy to discover the important role of Christians with a little research.

No, high intelligence does not make faith more difficult. A rebellious, defiant heart is the primary cause of unbelief. Self-focused egoism pushes God out of his place in the universe. I know this because I have often faced the realities of my own inner world.

A natural-born rebel, I shelter an astonishing capacity to tell my Creator to leave me alone so I can do as I please. Doubt is a convenient way to justify going my own way.

My proclivity for dishonest doubt nearly destroyed me. I excelled at using questions to avoid answers. So I know people can be good at putting God off indefinitely. And that brings me to my friend Tim.

Some people love their doubts.

When Tim first appeared in my life I immediately drafted him as a point guard for the church league basketball team. Some described him as a "scrapper" and a better-than-average shooter. We played well together for two seasons and won most of our games. A casual friendship developed that allowed me to invite him to church. He attended with his wife and his skepticism. After a few weeks, Tim asked if he could have a conversation with me. He said he had some questions about what he heard at church.

Though happy to meet with Tim, I felt apprehensive about his list of questions. He sounded a little too sure of himself when he mentioned it. When he arrived in my office, to my dismay, he carried a yellow legal pad covered with small print. Instinctively I knew I was in for a grilling. After some small talk about our victory in the basketball tournament, we got down to business.

Tim started. "I've been collecting questions about God, the Bible, and faith for several years." He flipped open the legal pad with several pages of single-spaced questions.

"Okay, let's start at the top," I said with mild anxiety. "What's your first question?"

"How do you know there is a God, and how do you know he's the real one?" he asked. Nothing like working into it gradually!

For the next two hours we went at it. He tried to punch holes in my faith with his tough, hard-nosed questions, and I offered the best answers I could. Along the way, he admitted it surprised him there were so many good answers. He also felt pleased I didn't have satisfactory explanations for all the issues he raised.

Finally I said, "Tim, something seems odd to me."

"What?"

"I noticed you came here with your questions carefully written out and arranged on paper, but you haven't written down any of the answers. You told me many of my answers impressed you as being good ones, yet you haven't written them down. Besides that, when you found out there was a reasonable answer, you immediately went on to your next question. What do you think that tells me?"

He looked a bit chagrined and shrugged, "I guess I'm a little over-enthusiastic about how clever I think I am."

I said, "No, that's not it. I'm beginning to suspect you are not really interested in the answers to your questions. You don't collect answers. You collect questions. I think you may be using your doubts and cynicism as a wall to keep God out of your life, or at least to keep him at a distance. I don't want to hurt your feelings, but my impression is that you actually are extremely fond of your list."

Tim grinned and admitted to some truth in my observations. He was not at all put out by my honesty. Instead, he challenged me. "Let's do this again, if you're up for it."

"Sure," I said. "Why don't you go back over your collection of questions and pick out the ones for which you need solid answers? This is great fun and I'll look forward to next time."

A week later Tim returned. This time the yellow legal pad was missing. I raised my eyebrows and asked the obvious: "Where are your questions?"

"I left them at home," he replied. "I have come to the conclusion you were right on target about loving questions but not answers. I'm here today to talk about what I do believe, not what I don't yet understand."

What followed was one of the most memorable journeys to faith

I ever had the privilege to witness. Tim steadily stepped into life under God's leadership. It didn't happen overnight. He did his due diligence with caution. But eventually Tim surrendered to Jesus, accepted forgiveness, and received the heavenly welcome-home embrace waiting for him.

We still reminisce about his infamous list of questions, and he laughs at how carefully he compiled it. He remembers feeling "absolutely sure" he'd uncovered all the questions Christians could not answer. He thought he could prove that nothing about biblical faith could be trusted. Instead, with time, he developed a love for answers, even though he still asks questions. The difference is astounding.

An inquiring mind and an open heart stir up faith! That's what happened to me and to Tim, and it's what can happen to you.

TWELVE

SEEING GOD

Born blind. Everything else works fine: hearing, speech, smell, taste, and an exceptional mind. But blind! He puzzles over the purpose of his limitation. Is begging in the streets all he was meant to do with his life? Day after day, wasting a good life in humiliation and hopeless poverty?

The blind beggar hears some strangers stop near him so he rattles his alms bowl to attract attention. They talk about him like a theological curiosity. Someone says, "Who sinned, this man or his parents that would have caused him to be born blind?"

Exactly, he thinks. *Welcome to my world of inexplicable unfairness.*

Then a voice of authority speaks with certainty: "Neither this man nor his parents sinned. This isn't about negative consequences for bad choices. Rather, he was born blind so God could one day show what he can do for him."

"Shh," someone says. "Jesus is saying something. I want to hear this."

Oh really! the blind man thinks. *I have asked God to open my eyes and let me see the world around me a million times. But nothing ever changes.*

The authoritative voice continues: "We must do what the One who sent me wants us to do while it is day. The night when no one can do anything is coming. As long as I am in the world, I light the world."

What an unusual speech, the blind man thinks. *A man claiming to be the source of light; now that's a new one!*

Then he hears someone spitting and feels a presence blocking the sun's heat. A strong hand firmly holds the back of his neck and the other hand gently smears something across his closed eyes. Usually no one touches him other than his parents, and usually they're leading him someplace. Yet the blind man doesn't fight the stranger's hold on him. He just fears becoming the laughing stock of the beggar community.

With a hand holding the beggar's head, the man's voice gently instructs, "Go wash it off in the pool of Siloam." Then the blind man is alone again with mud dripping down his cheeks. The blind man doesn't think mud will enhance his solicitations, so he probably asks his fellow beggar, Levi, to help him get down to Siloam. Levi's arms are shriveled, but he can see. With his hand on Levi's shoulder, they slowly walk to the pool and wash off the mud.

"Light! It must be. It can't be!" With a mud-free face, the blind man now sees.

A few minutes later he looks at his father and mother for the first time. Shocked, they weep and praise God. For the rest of that day, their son's eyes feast on the wonders around him.

As news of the miracle travels, neighbors arrive. But they find it difficult to believe his story. Is this really the blind man? Some neighbors want the Pharisees to weigh in on the amazing event, especially because Jesus healed him on the Sabbath, the Jewish day of rest.

The religious leaders act strangely offended. "The man who did this to you, this Jesus character, could not have been from God because he didn't follow the traditions for the Sabbath," they insist. Then an argument breaks out among them. Some can't make the same snap judgment. These dissenters ask, "Wait a minute, how can a man who is a sinner perform miracles like these?"

They turn back to the formerly blind man and ask, "What's your opinion about this man called Jesus who gave you sight?"

By this time the beggar concludes that not just anybody could open his eyes, and answers, "My best guess is he is a prophet."

The Pharisees figure it's a fabricated story, so they try to dismantle it. They call in the beggar's parents and ask, "Is this really your son and was he born blind? If so, why can he see now?"

His parents fear the religious leaders. They're swimming in dangerous waters of political correctness. Anyone who believes Jesus is the Messiah will be barred from the synagogue, an important privilege for devout Jews. So the parents play it as close to the vest as possible. "Yes, we know he's our son and he was born blind. But we don't know how he received his sight. He is of age, you'll have to ask him."

The Pharisees can't let it rest. They call back the man born blind. "Give glory to God alone," they command. "We are positive this man, who you think healed you, is a sinner and couldn't have been the source of your good fortune."

The formerly blind man sputters, "Look, I don't know if the man we are talking about is a sinner or not. But one thing I know. I used to be blind, but now I can see. Why can't you accept that amazing fact and rejoice with me?"

But they keep badgering him. He doesn't take their pressure sitting down and keeps answering boldly. Finally they lose patience and throw him out of the synagogue. The city buzzes with the story, and eventually Jesus hears about it.

Jesus looks for the man who is willing to be excommunicated

for standing up for his Healer. When he finds the man, Jesus asks, "Do you believe in the Son of Man, the Messiah?"

The man replies, "Sir, tell me who he is so I can believe in him." Jesus tells him, "You've seen him, the one who healed you and who is talking to you now. I am God's appointed deliverer."

The former blind man falls to his knees before Jesus, the eyes of his heart opened, and he says, "My Lord, I believe. I see you for who you really are!" (See John 9:1–38; adapted from the NIV.)

Seeing the true light is the result of the deepest healing.

The blind man's healing ranks as the longest miracle story in the New Testament. It contains profound theological questions and addresses the central issue of Jesus's identity. The main character struggles with blindness in two ways. He can't see sunlight physically. And he can't see the Light of the world spiritually.

However, the healed blind man progresses in his belief. He considers Jesus—first, a kind stranger; second, a prophet; third, a devout man approved by God; and finally, the eyes of his heart see Jesus as his Lord. His gradual move toward belief and spiritual sight models faith for us. Anyone can take this journey. We are all born blind to spiritual light. Our blindness can take various forms. Scripture says all have sinned (Rom. 3:23), which we each prove almost daily. But we all can walk, grope, or run toward God's Light, unless we shut it off by refusing to bow and believe.

Thinking metaphorically, the Pharisees represent people who refuse Jesus as God in a human body. For a variety of reasons, they just don't go there. They are religious; in fact, very religious. Unfortunately, they like to tell God what he can and cannot do. Theirs is a form of blindness called self-righteous pride. It is a kingdom of the ego that refuses healing. It is an addiction to man-made religion that surprisingly opposes the very God they profess.

The Blind Beggar
John 9

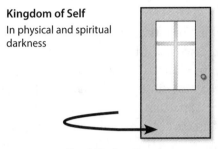

Kingdom of Self
In physical and spiritual darkness

Kingdom of God
• Found the light of the world: "Once I was blind but now I see."
• Works of God on display in his life

• "Lord, I believe."
• He worshiped Jesus
• Came to understand who Jesus was
• Healed in body and soul

The former blind man represents those who relentlessly follow spiritual light until they reach the Light of the World (John 8:12). Seeing with the heart takes them to the choice of acknowledging Jesus is Lord of all. Multitudes of people before and since have taken the same journey.

The blind man has modern counterparts.

God can transform agnostics and addicts like Jack Harris. Even though Jack learned about the Creator in Sunday school, a public high-school teacher explained a universe without God, and it made sense to him. A worldview free from religious rules and accountability felt like freedom, and Jack enthusiastically converted to agnosticism and its traveling partner, hedonism.

In short order, Jack fell head-over-heels in love with the pursuit of pleasure. Along with some friends, he threw off former restraints. Life morphed into one continuous party.

Surprisingly, in spite of considerable recreational drug use, he managed to finish college. Even with a serious alcohol problem, he acquired a decent job with a bright future. The money started rolling in.

Jack also moved in with a beautiful woman who shared his lifestyle. But one day he discovered her in bed with another man. She saw nothing wrong with it. He couldn't accept an open relationship and he moved out. But it wasn't that easy. Having previously studied domestic partnership law, she had insisted on putting ownership of assets in both their names: cars, furniture, house, credit cards, even retirement investments. Consequently, she wiped him out financially. Jack wound up broke and starting over.

In their final conversation, Jack's former girlfriend explained her commitment to herself and voiced her surprise he wasn't just like her. She explained, "You don't believe in God. You've thrown away your religious upbringing. You think the Bible is a bunch of crap, and you don't believe in moral principles unless they benefit you. You are committed to your own enjoyment of experiences and pleasure. So I'm just living your dream. Why shouldn't I sleep with whomever I want? Why shouldn't I take your money? Why shouldn't I do exactly as I please? I am just being true to myself. So grow up. Be consistent with your belief system. Everyone is selfish. Why on earth should that surprise or disappoint you?"

These words shook Jack. Something felt very wrong with her picture of reality. He didn't understand it intellectually, but his gut said he was headed in the wrong direction. Depression settled in, and he self-medicated with alcohol and painkillers. Watching Jack turn into a wreck, his boss told him to clean up his life or look for a new job. That finally got through to him. Jack liked his job and income. How could he get off this personal roller coaster rushing him toward disaster?

Calling darkness light is a common tactic.

Jack began meeting with a therapist. She helped lift his self-worth and self-image, at least for a while. But as he studied his notes and reviewed the reading material, he realized she wanted him to redefine everything.

"Who's to say what's real or true?" she often asked. "Why don't you set up a way of thinking that satisfies you?"

"Okay, so nothing is really good or evil, true or false, right or wrong?" he asked.

"That's it exactly!" she said enthusiastically. "What's messing your head up is other people's twisted thinking. What's good for you? What's right for you? You have to love yourself first."

"You mean it's all subjective? It's all whatever I want it to be? There is no baseline of reality?" he asked. He didn't like her response.

"You're getting it! This is a breakthrough." She was genuinely excited with his "progress."

Redefining, questioning, and turning everything upside down gave Jack a temporary shot in the arm. But eventually this process made him feel worse. A terrifying emotional and spiritual darkness closed in around him. He felt lost and hopeless in this process of building a worldview of no absolutes. He recognized he was no longer interested in the deconstruction of basic moral values.

Eventually Jack quit therapy and in desperation attended Alcoholics Anonymous to confront the alcohol abuse threatening to destroy the remaining shreds of his life. In AA he heard a different philosophy. The veterans of self-deception who called themselves "dry drunks" seemed amused by his recently acquired therapeutic jargon.

One old-timer named Harry said, "Pal, you have been led down the ramp into the cattle cars. Next is the shower with the sweet-smelling cyanide. Come on; wake up to the fact that constructing your own reality is another way of defining insanity!"

"You mean you believe in some kind of absolute standard of right and wrong?" asked Jack.

"Yup. To create your own standard is to set yourself up as your own higher power. In other words, you're playing God—and it's obvious that's not working for you, is it?"

Jack shook his head then buried his face in his hands. "I'm so confused," he mumbled. "There's no light at the end of my tunnel. It's dark, so very dark and depressing inside."

Harry waited patiently. "Okay, Jack, let's go over the first steps. It's time you admit you're helpless when it comes to your addiction. It's time to let go of the control center of your life and surrender everything to a higher power."

"What higher power? I don't believe in God. I don't believe in any higher authority than myself. I have nowhere to go with that idea," Jack lamented.

"Did you ever believe in God?"

"Sure, when I was a kid. I used to go to church with my parents and all that stuff. But I outgrew that fantasy."

Harry laughed. "Fantasy? You call living as if you are the one in charge reality? And the idea of God being in charge a fantasy? Think about it! You have really gone off the deep end."

Those comments jolted Jack. "You mean you think there's actually a God, a real higher power? Someone who should be allowed to tell us what to do? I don't know anyone besides my parents who still believe that."

"Okay, I see where you're coming from and I have to agree with you. It is dark in that tunnel of yours. No wonder you've been drowning yourself in Jack Daniels. But there's no light at the bottom of a bottle either, is there, my friend?" He put his hand on Jack's shoulder. "Here's my card. I'll be your sponsor. Call me anytime, day or night, if you need help staying sober. See you tomorrow night."

Harry left smiling. Jack took a long walk in the rain. Back in his bedroom, he couldn't sleep. Finally, Jack talked to God for the first time in years. "God, I guess I'm back to you. I can't see how you could possibly make a difference, but hey, it's worth a try. What have I got to lose? So here goes. I choose to submit to you as my higher power . . . and I don't even know if you're there." His voice trailed off in a whisper of longing for something or someone.

The light still dawns after all these years.

By the time Jack completed the twelve-step program through AA, he started getting his life back. The addiction to alcohol fell away. To the best of his ability, he surrendered personal control to God. Jack also structured his life. He discovered he could live sanely, responsibly, and thoughtfully. But he was still restless. Something was missing. He felt like a patient recovering from a coma who knew there must have been a doctor involved, but never actually met him.

One day Jack revealed his feelings to Harry. "Did you ever experience what I'm talking about? Did you ever wish you could know God personally and not just pragmatically use the idea of God?"

Harry looked at him for a long time and then asked, "Is it okay if I read something from the Bible?"

Jack said, "Sure, why not?"

Harry read the story of the blind man whose physical and spiritual eyes opened. When Harry closed the book, he asked, "Jack, what happened when the man born blind recognized Jesus was God?"

Jack stared at him with a sick feeling rising up inside. "Jesus is God, the real Higher Power? Is that what you're suggesting?"

Harry nodded. Jack shook his head and paced back and forth in consternation. "If that's the truth then my parents have been right all along. I've made a big circle. I've ended up where I started." He laughed and it sounded harsh.

Harry let the silence grow. Finally, he got up from the park bench and put the Bible in his backpack. As they walked toward the car he said, "One more thing. The healed blind man prayed a three-word prayer, 'Lord, I believe.' You might want to try it."

A few hours later Jack finally uttered the same three words to Jesus. He wasn't sure what would happen; he just knew he meant it.

Jack read and reread the blind man's story. Something strange and wonderful began to happen. He could see Jesus for who he was. The story came alive. It became his story.

Over time Harry, with the Holy Spirit's help, shed spiritual light on Jack's life. In the light of Jesus's identity, Jack opened his eyes to his need for God's kingdom. In that same light, he clearly faced his alcohol addiction. He gradually let go of his hedonistic kingdom and trusted God to guide his recovery.

Today Jack still attends AA. He and Harry sponsor desperate people, carbon copies of themselves when they first arrived at a meeting. Harry calls Jack "one of the clearest thinkers" he knows. Jack carries himself with quiet confidence and deep humility. He knows the difference between deception and truth, between spiritual darkness and light. Jesus is his Lord and the source of his inner sight.

After Jack surrendered his kingdom, he discovered the apostle Paul's advice to the church at Ephesus: "We come to God as sinners; but He wants to transform our habits, attitudes, and practices into the ways of Jesus: to live, forgive, and love as He did. So imitate God. Follow Him like adored children, and live in love as the Anointed One loved you—so much that He gave Himself as a fragrant sacrifice, pleasing God" (Eph. 5:1–2 VOICE).

Jack and the biblical blind man found the door to repentant faith and entered the kingdom of light. The change was more than they could have hoped for.

You may have tried building a life without God that ended up in darkness. Before you join those who conveniently conclude that darkness is actually light, before you become a spiritual cynic, consider Jack's story. What if Jesus is "the true light that gives light to everyone" (John 1:9)? Self-imposed darkness is not courageous. It wastes your one and only life.

THIRTEEN

READY TO MEET GOD

Two of the most violent criminals in US history were Ted Bundy and Jeffrey Dahmer. Bundy preyed on girls and women; Dahmer on boys and men. Both violent sex addicts gave themselves wholly over to dark compulsions. They murdered dozens of innocent people to gratify out-of-control lust. Law enforcers eventually caught and convicted these men, but only after reigns of terror and death.

The state of Florida executed Ted Bundy in 1989 at age 42. A fellow prisoner bludgeoned Dahmer to death in 1994 while he served a life sentence. Dahmer was 34. These two monsters shared another characteristic in common: they both professed Jesus Christ as Savior and Lord. They received his forgiveness while in prison.

Many of us would exclaim, "No way!"

I did. How can such miserable excuses for human beings be let off the hook by a just God? If this is true that means even Adolf Hitler, Joseph Stalin, Mao Tse-tung, and Pol Pot could have repented and God would have forgiven them. That's entirely too much grace and mercy in my book!

Such unmerited and massive forgiveness feels unfair and impossible to believe, but it's consistent with biblical accounts of Jesus's character and teachings. He lives by a different book than we do. Even when put to death unjustly, he still forgives.

This is a tale of two thieves and a crucified king.

On Golgotha, a hill outside the walls of Jerusalem, the Romans regularly execute convicted felons and political prisoners. Using crucifixion, they nail people to wooden crosses and let them die slow, gruesome deaths. Because Jesus's message threatens the status quo of their religion, Jewish leaders convince the Romans to crucify him as a blasphemer who threatens the community's peace. So they collaborate to kill this wise, compassionate, and truly good man alongside common criminals.

In a remarkable coincidence, the soldiers nail a thief on each side of Jesus. One robber reviles, curses, and hurls insults at him. "Some Messiah you are! Save yourself and us!" In other words, he says, "If you are who you say you are, then act like it. You may think you're a teacher of righteousness, but you are just like the rest of us. We may be thieves but you're an imposter, a charlatan, and a fraud. If you really are the Christ, the God-man, you wouldn't be nailed to a Roman cross. You'd be running the whole show!"

Then the other thief does a strange thing. He parts company with his fellow criminal and says, "Don't you fear God? You and I are getting the same as him. We deserve this, but not him. He did nothing to justify how he is being treated."

Then he turns to Jesus and acknowledges him as King. "Jesus, remember me when you enter your kingdom." What an unusual place to surrender. Hanging on a cross, about to die, the thief places his faith in the leader of everything. (See Luke 23:39–43; adapted from the MSG.)

How does this hardened felon learn Jesus is the King of the

eternal kingdom of God? Most likely, he hears the buzz as the population talks about this new firebrand preacher and his kingdom message. Perhaps he stands and listens with the crowds following Jesus. Maybe a cellmate in prison knows about the popular rabbi from Galilee. With endless hours in lockup, the thief has time to discuss, speculate, and argue about this controversial public figure.

Or even more likely, for the repentant thief, it comes together at Calvary when he realizes who hangs beside him. He hears Jewish leaders taunting and sneering, "He saved others. Let's see if he can save himself." They suggest if he comes down from the cross it would prove he is, indeed, the Christ or Messiah promised by the prophets.

The repentant thief watches soldiers hang a sign above the head of Jesus. "This is the King of the Jews," it says. Pilate ordered it put there to goad the Jewish leaders for insisting on putting Jesus to death. The soldiers mock and mistreat him. "Come on, big shot. If you really are the King of the Jews like the sign says, prove it—save yourself!"

The thief cannot miss the unexpected cry of Jesus. With nails driven through his hands and feet, his face swollen and bruised from multiple beatings, his upper torso whipped to bloody ribbons, with a gruesome crown of thorns jammed down on his brow as someone's idea of a joke, Jesus cries out, "Father, forgive them, for they do not know what they are doing!"

It's possible such mercy tips the scales for the bandit as it has for countless others through the centuries. *Here's a man I can admire and respect. Here's a leader I can trust and follow. A good God would be like this. I'm going to take a chance. I'm going for it.* Turning to his partner in suffering, the thief calls his name, "Jesus?" The battered face turns; the bloodshot swollen slits for eyes fasten on him.

"Please remember me when you come into your kingdom!" At death's door, the criminal recognizes the Lord of All and asks for inclusion in his eternal kingdom.

Maybe Jesus smiles. It would be like him, although it probably looks more like a grimace. Then he promises, "Today you will be with me in paradise." (See Luke 23:32–43; adapted from the NIV.)

The Bandit on the Cross
Luke 23:39–43

Kingdom of Self
• Doing whatever it took to get what he wanted
• Making his own rules

Kingdom of God
"Today you will be with me in paradise."

• "Don't you fear God?"
• Recognized Jesus as the king of God's kingdom
• Asked to be included

Of the two criminals, it's still easier to identify with the cynical skeptic. Jesus certainly does not appear to be in charge of anything. Hanging on the cross, he looks like a deluded, perhaps even deranged, do-gooder ground under by the wheels of power, more to be pitied than feared. Not even a desperate criminal would normally believe Jesus was God, yet that's what the second bandit does. He believes, recognizes his King, and receives forgiveness and the assurance that he now belongs to the kingdom.

The fog on our glasses comes from within.

Regarding Jesus, people today draw the same conclusions as the unbelieving thief. With the world in constant crisis, it doesn't look like Jesus is much of a leader or that following him makes sense. Other kingdoms seem more impressive. Other kings appear far more influential and powerful. Here's why: instead of immediate political results, God's kingdom focuses on inner changes and eternal impact.

Accordingly, people looking at him allow the eyes of their hearts to open. They see past the surface layer and catch sight of God's invisible but very present kingdom. Pride and preoccupation with self tends to fog our spiritual lenses and we can overlook God's spiritual kingdom entirely. But wipe away the fog, and we identify unbelievable but welcome forgiveness.

The in-the-nick-of-time thief resembles others who meet the Master. Like the rest of us, he struggles with lifelong control issues and rebellious sin. Yet he literally accepts eternal life at the last minute on the cross. When Christ's sacrificial love rips open salvation's door, this forgiven rebel steps through. He's the first to joyfully enter God's paradise with his newfound King at his side.

The thief can't harbor illusions about bringing anything to the table. He is morally bankrupt, caught red-handed, tried and convicted. He is at the end of his rope, and Jesus purchases his entrance to eternal life in the kingdom as a gift of love and mercy. There was nothing the thief could do but accept the gift.

But stop for a moment and think about this. Did this man take a shortcut, living life as he pleased up until the last moment and then accepting forgiveness? According to Jesus, everyone enters the kingdom the same way, with belief and repentance. It can happen at any time during someone's life, even up to the last minute. It's never too late.

The Bible insists that God "is patient with you, not wanting anyone to perish, but everyone to come to repentance" (2 Peter 3:9). For us, it might seem unfair that the word *anyone* applies here. After all, how can some be faithful followers for a lifetime while others confess late and get the same benefits? This is the depth, breadth, and mystery of God's unfathomable goodness and grace. This love exceeds our own.

But confession, early or late, must be sincere.

In a cardiac surgery unit in a big city hospital, Reggie endured open-heart surgery. He occupied a bed in the intensive care facility, but the last-ditch effort to save his life was failing. Reggie was dying and only machines kept him alive. Nancy called and asked me to hurry to the hospital to pray with her husband. Less than thirty minutes later I stood at his bedside.

"Thanks for coming," Reggie said with difficulty. "I'm sure it's no secret why I want you here. I'm ready to get right with God." He took several deep breaths and continued, "Please help me say the words and pray the prayer."

A self-made man, Reggie deliberately had kept his distance from God. Despite his wife's and children's active faith, he resisted. Now Nancy sat in the corner of his room sobbing quietly. Under these circumstances, with her husband fighting for every breath, I led him in a prayer of repentance. He repeated each phrase after me, and asked Jesus to forgive him for taking God's place and for running his own life. He asked Jesus to take over whatever was left of his life.

Even though Reggie completed the prayer, the situation troubled me deeply. A few minutes later, he died. After Nancy's immediate expressions of grief, I asked why she appeared disturbed while I led her husband to faith and repentance. I'll never forget what she said.

"Reggie always told me he was going to live his life his way as long as he could. Then before he died he would take advantage of God's salvation through Jesus and get set up for the next life."

She paused for a long moment, gazing out the window and then continued, "He always took pride in figuring out the system and playing it to his best advantage. I'm sad because I just don't think anyone can manipulate God like that. I know it's the unconditional grace of God that's involved, but Reggie wasn't humble and genuinely submissive just now when he prayed with you. I know him too well to be mistaken about that."

Nancy tried to hold back tears, but broke into racking sobs. "Jan," she cried, "he was gloating as he died. He thought he had beaten the system and cut a sweet last-minute deal."

At that point I understood what I sensed in my uneasy spirit during Reggie's deathbed confession of faith. Reggie assumed the right prayer would get him through heaven's door. He thought using the right words in the right order would trip the cosmic lock on the door to the kingdom. His faith in a magic salvation prayer missed the reality of true repentance.

What a contrast between the repentant robber on his cross and Reggie's departure! One man sincerely understood and repented late. The other worked the system until the last possible minute. I do not recommend Reggie's path.

Being locked in with a Hell's Angel made a huge difference.

No matter anyone's sin, it's not too late to repent and receive God's forgiveness. Carl is a good example. He's a convict serving hard time in a federal penitentiary for rape and pedophilia. Before incarceration, he developed a vile bondage to pornography, prostitution, and the sexual molestation of children.

Carl also felt nothing but resentment, contempt, and rage toward Christianity, and for good reason. Years earlier, a religious leader in his family's church introduced him to pornographic magazines, videos, and homosexual sex. Because Carl is a repeat offender, the penal system considers him hardened and incorrigible.

Then last year Carl observed a remarkable change in his Hell's Angel cellmate and decided to join the Bible study he attended. After three months of listening, learning, and discussing, Carl personally met the God who died a criminal's death to offer guilty people pardon.

For the first time Carl realized his sin against God and others.

Up until then he thought his only regrettable mistake was getting caught. Now he recognized the ugliness of his obsession with selfish needs, desires, and pleasures. Then the incomprehensible happened; he repented in deep sorrow and gave control of his life to Jesus as Savior and King. Carl is changing. He's becoming a new man, something the rehabilitation experts say is impossible. Slowly he is developing dignity and self-respect for the first time in his life. This convicted sexual predator is becoming a sane, likeable man, experiencing freedom from his obsessions and addictions.

God can and does take anyone who repents in genuine humility. He extends a choice. We can keep our distance, or we can close the gap by admitting we need his forgiveness and leadership.

You might be thinking, "But I'm not that bad!"

What makes a person bad enough to deserve hell or good enough to enter heaven? Do certain heinous crimes cancel our chances of entering the door to peace? Does a life of doing good tilt the determination in our favor? Many think in terms of a balancing scale, with our good deeds on one side and bad deeds on the other. If we think our good deeds outweigh our bad deeds, we feel positive about our chances of getting into heaven.

That way of thinking makes logical sense, but it doesn't represent what Jesus thought and taught. He considered playing God, pushing him out of the driver's seat and taking his place, the worst sin of all. All other sins are symptoms of that sin. This universal crime against heaven is so commonplace, so normal, we don't think of it as wrong. We admire independent, self-sufficient, wanting-my-own-way people. But should we?

We place ourselves in a different category from mass murderers and sexual predators when we rank sin against people differently than sin against God. Jesus corrects that erroneous thinking by calling all people to repentance, with no exceptions and no differences. Ted Bundy, Jeffrey Dahmer, Adolf Hitler, you, and I all equally need God's mercy and forgiveness. Jesus allows no room for the "I'm too bad" or "I'm too good" attitude. In front of the door to peace at the cross the ground levels. We deny ourselves entrance when we imagine our sin is not bad enough to need so severe a remedy.

FOURTEEN

GIVING UP TO GOD

The Bible describes Zacchaeus as curious and short, with a bad reputation (see Luke 19:1–10). Curiosity draws him into the crowd gathered around Jesus. His height compels him to climb a sycamore tree to see and hear the Teacher. But the tree does more than just make Jesus easier to see. It also makes the little man stand out. Jesus walks up and says, "Zacchaeus, come down immediately. I must stay at your house today" (v. 5).

Imagine that: the celebrity teacher everyone talks about wants to visit his house! Zacchaeus scrambles down and gladly welcomes Jesus into his home. Watching this, people mutter, "What business does he have getting cozy with this crook?" (v. 7 MSG). Zacchaeus's community views him, a chief tax collector, as a turncoat collaborator with Roman occupational forces. They regard him as a social parasite, preying on his own people for selfish advantage.

Tax gatherers, or publicans, collect what the Roman government demands then keep what they extort for themselves. The Jewish population hates this arrangement, which amounts to legal robbery backed by the Roman army. In essence, Jews regard tax collectors as scum, the lowest dregs of the community. Obvious sinners.

Scripture doesn't record what Jesus teaches while Zacchaeus listens with the crowd, or the conversation during lunch in the tax collector's home. But given the pattern of the New Testament gospels, they probably talk about the kingdom of God and repentance. In response, Zacchaeus promises, "Here and now I give half of my possessions to the poor, and if I have cheated anybody out of anything, I will pay back four times the amount" (v. 8).

Imagine the shock rippling through the household and into the streets. "The tax man's gone crazy! He is giving his ill-gotten gains to the poor and paying back the money he extorted—with interest! Can you believe it? Can a zebra change his stripes or a leopard her spots? This is a miracle."

That's exactly how Jesus viewed this remarkable turnaround. He said, "Today salvation has come to this house, because this man, too, is a son of Abraham. For the Son of Man came to seek and to save the lost" (vv. 9–10).

There's power in a captivating vision.

How do we interpret this story twenty centuries later? Does Zacchaeus buy his way into heaven? Does he pay for the forgiveness he needs? Is this possible? Of course not. Nobody can bribe a holy, truly good God.

The facts indicate Zacchaeus repents. The tax collector recognizes Jesus's divinity and does the only sensible thing: he surrenders his kingdom. At that point, Zacchaeus knows what to do next. Although he lied, cheated, and stole to accumulate his fortune, wealth no longer motivates him. While talking to Jesus, he glimpses something better, something of far higher value—the kingdom of God. In view of a new vision of eternal value, he now regards his ill-gotten gains as expendable.

He figures, "Why not off-load the money? It contaminates my life. And besides, repayment is the right thing to do." Because of his power and wealth, he attends the right parties and social events, along with his Roman masters. The Jewish power class includes him, but then these same leaders sneer behind his back. Now after talking with Jesus, he doesn't care. For the first time, Zacchaeus feels free. He can hold up his head in the Synagogue, the Jewish house of worship.

This awakening to what is truly valuable suggests Zacchaeus's success with get-rich-quick schemes has never actually satisfied him. For years he works the system to his advantage while feeling ashamed of himself. He thinks everyone wants money, so why not get his share of the pie? Then he meets Jesus and discovers a kingdom that fully satisfies the longings of his heart.

The Tax Collector: *Zacchaeus*
Luke 19:1–10

Kingdom of Self
- Wealth
- Possessions
- Prominence
- Power

Kingdom of God
- "Today salvation has come to this house."
- Generosity
- Restitution

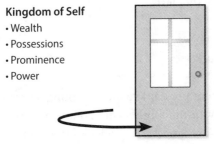

- Sell what you have, give it to the poor
- Come, follow me

A massive change of heart like Zacchaeus's can only originate through Jesus. He is the door, the authority, the powerful Name that allows entrance into God's kingdom. The tax collector's newfound generosity and restitution, shocking in a man who previously put himself first, affirms his heart is being transformed. He willingly is relaxing under God's reign. He abandons his temporary wealth for an unshakable kingdom nobody can take from him.

Jesus tells two short stories that dial Zacchaeus into perspective. He says, "God's kingdom is like a treasure hidden in a field for years and then accidentally found by a trespasser. The finder is ecstatic—what a find!—and proceeds to sell everything he owns to raise money and buy that field. Or, God's kingdom is like a jewel merchant on the hunt for excellent pearls. Finding one that is flawless, he immediately sells everything and buys it" (Matt. 13:44–46 MSG).

Jesus is defining intelligent behavior for the spiritually hungry. God's kingdom measures a person's value system, not mental agility or business savvy. The kingdom of God provides genuine value. After learning about God's kingdom, holding on to a personal kingdom defines spiritual suicide. Operating from the kingdom of personal control, we mistake pennies for hundred dollar bills and hundred dollar bills for pennies. Jesus insists the kingdom of God offers immense value that lasts.

What are you looking for?

Brent is the most affluent person I've met. A young owner of a cellular phone company, he quickly became a billionaire. Brent loved the fast pace, pressure, and cutting edge of the high-tech world. He owned a summer home on Hood Canal with a panoramic view of the Olympic Mountains, a winter chalet in Austria, and an 8,000-square-foot home on a new PGA golf course. He played with all the toys: cars, boats, motorcycles, and a personal jet. But when I met him, he still restlessly searched for something more.

A friend connected me to Brent after he decided to pursue spirituality. In the same way this CEO researched business deals, he investigated religious options. I was fourth on his interview list. Brent had already looked into Buddhism, Islam, and Christian Science. When he invited me to his home, we sat in creamy brown leather chairs overlooking the Hood Canal of Puget Sound. I wondered what God would prompt me to say to a man who had accumulated more money than I could imagine.

I asked Brent, "What are you looking for?"

"The best deal I can find. I am comparing the benefits in this life and the kind of heaven that's offered in the next life." He was serious.

I felt sympathy for Brent, who had built a large, yet somehow unfulfilling personal kingdom. I explained the lasting benefits of living for a resurrected Lord instead of money. He understood. But the reality of God's kingdom stung and irritated him, raising his anxiety level. He could not escape the logic of surrender to God's kingdom and authority. However, he could not avoid the implications of submission to his leadership. Brent immediately assessed the cost of entering the heavenly kingdom. Understandably, it felt like a huge threat to his carefully constructed kingdom.

Over time, after several dialogues about the Bible, we encountered Zacchaeus. Brent's reaction didn't surprise me. "This is exactly what I was afraid of," he said. "In my gut I knew getting my life straightened out with God would look something like it did for the tax guy. That scares me."

As Brent paced in front of a window, he desperately tried to find a way to keep his kingdom, stay in control of his life, and tack on the benefits of a faith relationship with Jesus.

Finally I said, "Brent, you can't find a way around repentance. There isn't any other way to enter the kingdom of God." I paused. "Suppose Bill Gates offered you his kingdom in exchange for yours, would you be interested?"

"That's a no-brainer. I'd be turning my billion into his megabillions," he replied, stuffing his hands in his pockets.

"Okay, then why can't you open your tightly closed hands to the CEO of the entire universe in exchange for his love, generosity, and incredible resources? Even if Bill Gates is currently one of the richest men in the world, what he owns is insignificant compared with what's available under the leadership of Jesus."

Brent sat down on the edge of his chair. "That's a good illustration. I guess my cell phone company is a kingdom. I've given it my full allegiance for ten years, and it's been good to me. But I can't imagine letting go of what I have in my hands for just the promise of something better. It's too much for God to ask of me."

"Brent, how long do you think you'll be able to possess and control your kingdom?"

He thought about my question for a few moments, leaning back in his chair. "I suppose until I die. Okay, I see your point. I'm going to lose control eventually anyway, no matter what I do. I'll have to pass on my stuff to my kids or to some bird sanctuary. But you're right; I can't take it with me."

"The amazing thing is, according to Jesus, you can send it on ahead!" I said. "Listen to this." I picked up my Bible and turned to the conclusion of the rich young ruler's story (which we looked at in chapter 3). I read aloud: "'Truly I tell you,' Jesus replied, 'no one who has left home or brothers or sisters or mother or father or children or fields for me and the gospel will fail to receive a hundred times as much in this present age: homes, brothers, sisters, mothers, children and fields—along with persecutions—and in the age to come eternal life. But many who are first will be last, and the last first'" (Mark 10:29–31).

I looked up. "Brent, you can keep what you have and stay stubbornly in control for now and lose it all, including entrance into heaven, the place where God's kingdom is the only reality. Or you can sign over the management of your life to the Lord Jesus. If you live for him and serve him, you will have absolute confidence about where you will go when you die. It's your choice."

We often try to negotiate a better deal.

Brent took a long drink and irritably clinked the ice in his glass. "Look, I went to a church school when I was a kid. I know something about this stuff. Why can't I just accept Jesus as my Savior and have my sins forgiven? I thought the Christian message was about accepting the gift of God's love."

I admired his persistence. "So you want to add Jesus and forgiveness and heaven to your kingdom? Sounds to me like you don't like God's terms and are trying to negotiate a better deal."

He grimaced. "I guess that is what I'm doing, isn't it? Well, you can't blame me for trying, can you?" His frown turned to a hopeful smile.

"Let me explain this before I go," I said. "All we're talking about is your return to the intended order of things. God designed you to function at your maximum potential within his kingdom. When you stay outside his original purpose, reentry to God's way of life seems scary."

I continued. "I just want to state the obvious: God doesn't need your pile of stuff. He wants you. Your heart aligned with his. He has no intention of arbitrarily pulling rank and making your life miserable by forcing you to do things that don't fit who you are. When you hand over your life in its entirety to him, he doesn't strip you. Rather, you become a shareholder under his management. Your life becomes part of his kingdom, and you are responsible and accountable to your Leader for how it is used. When God reigns in the throne room of your heart, his kingdom arrives in your personal world."

"I'm beginning to understand why Jesus said what he said. It makes sense," Brent acknowledged. He paused, stared at an eagle soaring over the trees, and asked, "So what should I do next?"

"Surrender—open your heart and hands. Jesus opened access to God's kingdom. From the human perspective it looks like he was executed for stirring up political unrest. But from the divine viewpoint, he took the consequences of our selfishness and rebellion upon himself. He pardoned us by taking our place in the courtroom of God's perfect justice."

Brent blurted out, "So that's how it works!"

I felt like giving him a high five, but I kept talking. "Are you ready to make that exchange?"

"How?" Brent whispered, his eyes moist. His face tightened with emotion.

"The most natural way is to pray. Tell God what he's been waiting to hear from you for a long time."

"Now? Right here?" I sensed Brent felt uncomfortable with prayer.

"Sure. You don't need special words or a formula. Just talk to God like you were talking to me. He'll hear you."

I waited quietly during a long pause.

Brent finally leaned forward in the chair, holding his head in his hands.

"Well, here goes," he said. "God? I'm really new at this. I've been running the show in my world as long as I can remember. I'm beginning to realize I took over your job. I'm really sorry. It was pretty arrogant of me now that I think about it. Thanks for not giving up on me. There's part of me that is kicking and screaming and part of me that is so excited I can hardly stand it. I want to, uh, I guess—man this is hard—formally ask you to take over my life. From now on it's all yours and I'm yours. There, I never thought I would be able to say that and mean it—but I do. I want you to be my leader and I want your kingdom more than anything else. Please help me follow through with this."

Brent looked up at me. "How do I end this?"

"Just say, 'Amen.' It means, 'so be it.'"

"Amen."

A few years after Brent's life-changing decision he retired from his successful career to give full-time attention to a Christian organization that teaches computer skills to businessmen in developing countries. And day by day, to individual after individual, he tells his story. He says when he accepted God's way, he gained everything. He never knew such fulfillment until he transferred his life's ownership to Jesus.

Jesus invites you to follow him too. You may already feel a stirring in your heart. If so, you can follow Brent's example and talk to God. He wants to hear from you. Tell him where your selfishness and preoccupation with control have taken you. Ask for his forgiveness and a clean, forgiven heart. Then give him everything. Welcome his loving leadership now and forever with no holdouts. That's genuine Christianity. That's true wealth.

FIFTEEN

RESPECT FOR GOD

A common fallacy says faith is a private thing. Nobody needs to know what we believe. Even more off base is the idea many people have that assumes all varieties of faith hold the same value. Jesus did not share that viewpoint. He drew a line from his kingdom gospel to the faith that attracts God's attention. Yet many kinds of faith surround us.

Unexamined faith. Ingrid's parents brought her up in the dominant religion of their community. Although Ingrid has never thought deeply about her faith, she says she "has always believed" since childhood. At age twenty-eight she's never attended any church other than her own. She's not read the Bible or a book about faith. While religion ingrains her life, she's never actively searched for God at a heart level. Why should she? Ingrid believes she's already found him.

Passively, Ingrid follows the rules of her denominational subculture, regularly observing its rituals. It's an activity practiced with her friends and family. Religion is part of her culture like patriotism, music, or food. Ingrid's faith in God follows a social pattern. Unfortunately, she will probably die without ever examining it.

Mental assent. Barry attended church schools from preschool through college. He possesses an excellent knowledge of biblical data, church history, and the multiple options offered by different Christian denominations. He loves to argue theology and discuss worldviews. He bases his faith on a mental memory bank. But on a practical level, he lives no differently than his faith-less neighbors. His faith does not impact his values, priorities, or personal agenda. Barry regards his Christianity as an interesting hobby. He happens to collect religious data like others specialize in Civil War trivia or old movies. He enjoys religion as a harmless, wholesome pastime.

Faith in faith. Olivia Stevens-Bond, a matriarch in her city, has long championed the arts and serves on the board of the largest hospital in town. The new hospice bears her name, honoring her tireless crusade for care of the dying. Mrs. Bond considers herself a practical Christian, though she rarely attends church.

Her favorite theological motto (accepted in her hospice care circles) is "all you have to do is have faith." After all, good works speak her faith. It doesn't matter upon whom or what the faith rests. She considers faith therapeutic. That makes it valuable. She considers the focus of faith a relatively minor issue.

In fact, any attempt to analyze or evaluate the legitimacy of various god options invites Olivia's wrath and a charge of discrimination and intolerance. In her worldview, humans are the masters. Faith is just one more useful tool to utilize for emotional well-being.

Faith as magic. Ben serves in the US Navy. He joined after high school, seriously considering a military career. The people who live and work with him don't know he thinks of himself as Christian. In fact, his life seems very much like that of his unbelieving friends. Ben would shock them if he admitted he attends church. Ben believes he is "saved" because he prayed a salvation prayer and received baptism at church during his junior year.

Some people place their faith in the right belief system, the right church, the right rituals, even the right words in the right order in the right prayer. They believe praying "the prayer" trips the cosmic lock and meets the minimum requirement for access to heaven. This approach resembles the incantation patterns of sorcery. Faith as magic usually doesn't make more than a superficial difference in lifestyles. It focuses on a mechanism-like ritual, something that zaps people in. This kind of faith avoids surrendering to God in repentance and embracing his ultimate authority. And it doesn't make a real difference in people's choices.

There is a man who expressed the kind of faith Jesus praised above all others . . .

We don't know if Jesus actually meets the Roman centurion face-to-face. They may only communicate through intermediaries, like two people who meet on the Internet and correspond by email. And yet Jesus pays the centurion the greatest honor he bestows on a Gentile.

This centurion serves as a career officer in charge of the primary unit of one hundred Roman soldiers. As a Roman officer in Israel, the Jews usually treat him with disdain and hostility. He is a hated foreign invader. But surprisingly, this man wins the respect and friendship of the Capernaum community where his garrison is stationed.

When the centurion asks Jesus to heal his servant, he understands the magnitude of his request. "Lord," he says, "I do not deserve to have you come under my roof. But just say the word, and my servant will be healed. For I myself am a man under authority, with soldiers under me. I tell this one, "Go," and he goes; and that one, "Come," and he comes. I say to my servant, "Do this," and he does it.' When Jesus heard this, he was amazed and said to those following him, 'Truly I tell you, I have not found anyone in Israel with such great faith'" (Matt. 8:8–10).

Take a closer look at this centurion. What does he do to elicit so strong a response from Jesus? Why does Jesus award him such high marks?

The centurion arrives with a desperate need, just like many others. Whether with leprosy, blindness, palsy, demon possession, or an empty religious heart, each carries his own expectations and agendas to Jesus. But the centurion approaches Jesus on behalf of another, a household servant he loves. Jesus recognizes him as a rare man who cares about the people he leads.

Notice how he approaches Jesus. Custom says if someone sends an emissary, it's the same as delivering the message yourself. In Luke's corresponding account of this story (7:1–10) that's exactly what he does. The centurion approaches Jesus through the city's elders, in the established protocol for seeking an audience with a king. He respectfully uses the line of Jewish authority to communicate with Jesus.

But again, why did Jesus praise this man for his faith? Because of his grasp of how authority and submission should function given the true identity of Jesus.

Was this really faith?

This Gentile soldier is a God-seeker. Intent on knowing the true God, in Jesus he recognizes ultimate authority. He figures if Jesus matches his claims, he holds power over life and death. Therefore, the centurion reasons that Jesus can heal anyone, anywhere, anytime.

Jesus calls this *great faith*. He enthusiastically approves the centurion's respect for authority, and this uncovers something important. Jesus wants allegiance. Yes, he saves souls, fulfills needs, and heals hurts. Certainly he restores the centurion's servant. But the highest concern for Jesus? That each of us becomes a citizen of his kingdom. In the kingdom we safely operate under his authority in the circle of his love.

The Military Officer
Luke 7:1–10

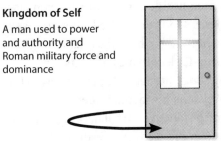

Kingdom of Self
A man used to power and authority and Roman military force and dominance

Kingdom of God
- Amazement of Jesus: "I have not found such great faith even in Israel."
- Recognition by Jesus of faith that expresses humility before God

- Considered himself unworthy
- Believed Jesus was God, treated him accordingly

Like many in authority, the centurion could easily have capitalized on his importance. Instead, he turns toward God, even before he meets Jesus. He clearly must have heard about Jesus's public speaking, healing, and miracles. Apparently that was enough for the centurion to be convinced to give the Master his allegiance.

Are you a man or woman "under authority"?

I'm not asking if you believe in Jesus, even though that's the place to start. But supposing you do believe in Jesus, are you practicing genuine, life-changing faith that restores God to his place as Supreme Authority in your life? If you're attempting to gain Christ's salvation without resolving the basic kingdom issue of governance, you've misunderstood faith. Christ's journey to the cross and his resurrection provide the entrance into God's kingdom, but not just onto its doorstep. Jesus intends to restore non-followers to active follower status.

This makes sense. The God of heaven and earth doesn't want to perpetuate the rebellion that cost him immeasurable pain and the death of his beloved Son. In fact, when we are genuinely reconciled to God, he transforms us from hostile competitors to team players. The life and death of Jesus, God's designated King, solves the authority problem we inherit from birth. In the kingdom of God every citizen gladly serves under legitimate authority.

If you still run the show, don't hesitate to humbly bow before the maker of all things. Welcome his loving leadership. Let him turn your life into a safe and productive part of his kingdom. This is repentant faith and the solution to chronic restlessness.

All that glitters is not gold.

Marv considers himself a player, a competitive person with guts, drive, and ambition. He loves being in control of his life, business, and family. His gorgeous wife, Claire, loves Marv, and he reigns like a king in his domain. He manages to run his personal agenda without hurting many people.

Living with Marv has pushed Claire past her limits, however. In desperation, she turned to God rather than a divorce attorney. That was almost five years ago. Years during which Claire has prayed that Marv would give his life to Jesus. The first time Claire had shared her new faith with Marv, he abruptly left the room in disgust. Since then, he'd barely tolerated her involvement with a church. "Religion," he sneered, "is a crutch for weak people." But through Claire, the kingdom of God had been residing under Marv's nose, sharing his home, waiting to burst into his self-contained bubble.

In recent months, Marv's carefully orchestrated world fell apart. First, his reliable instincts failed him. His trust in a new business partner proved to be a serious error in judgment. For the first time, his plan didn't work. He watched his hard-earned money start evaporating.

When he went to his yearly physical, the doctor detected a diminishing of strength on the right side of his body. A battery of expensive tests offered no conclusive answer. His doctor made an appointment for him to visit a specialist to discuss the possibility of multiple sclerosis. Marv's emotions ranged from intense anger and fear to a growing sense of helplessness and depression.

For the first time, Marv thought about God as if he really existed. He talked to him, but in anger: "Why? Why me? Why now? If you're trying to get my attention, okay, you've got it. So what do you want from me?"

Marv's long-cherished illusion of self-sufficiency met the inevitable realities of life. His carefully constructed and maintained kingdom crumbled. This strong-willed man stood at the threshold of a new way of life. Could he permit God to actually rule his life?

God works to get our attention.

Early one morning Claire woke up around two o'clock. Marv was not in bed. Claire put on her robe and looked for her husband. She found him sitting in a recliner, crying. She put her arms around him and softly explained the reality of following Jesus. As he listened, the light broke through his disappointment and self-pity.

It suddenly made sense to him. No question about it, he was well aware he resisted God. "What on earth have I been doing, Claire?" he asked. "I've been so completely preoccupied with myself. I haven't made room for God, or you, for that matter. What can I do? Tell me what you did that made so much difference. I've been watching, you know. You're a much better version of yourself now than when we got married."

The couple walked to the kitchen where she made hot cocoa. Then she joined him at the table and said, "Honey, all I did, all I could do was just give up trying to live life on my own. I asked for forgiveness for my preoccupation with myself and for my avoidance of God's leadership. I knew something about Jesus dying on the cross to pay for the consequences of sin, so I thanked him for setting that up for me. Then I said, 'God take over. I'm yours now. I accept your offer of forgiveness through your Son, Jesus.'"

That night Marv held his wife in his arms and accepted Jesus and his kingdom in repentant faith. He handed over the keys to his cherished kingdom of self, stepped through the door to peace, and entered the eternal kingdom of his Savior and new leader.

At his appointment with the specialist the next day, Marv learned he did not have a life-threatening illness, merely a pinched nerve in his back! But he did not renege on his new commitment.

Marv openly acknowledges that God's timing was impeccable. "A day later," he reluctantly admits, "I probably would not have been approachable or willing to listen."

Is the timing right?

God orchestrated events in Marv's life to give him the best possible chance to repent and embrace Jesus's kingdom reign. Perhaps this account reflects a similar pattern in your life. Reading this book at this time is no accident. Right now God may be maneuvering everything possible in your world to get your attention.

God has always been available to you, waiting and loving you across the distance you've created by insisting on your way. As you've considered the good news about Jesus, he's spoken loud and clear. You can close the distance. Accept God the Father's offer of pardon and enter into his kingdom through the door of forgiveness opened for us at the cross. Ask him for the faith to believe and humbly repent. Change your mind about who controls your heart.

Talk to God. He's waiting for you to choose sincere faith.

SIXTEEN

COMING TO GOD

Without exception Jesus pours his amazing love and compassion on humble, broken, oppressed people who seek him. In Scripture he treats them with gentleness and dignity. He refers to them as "poor in spirit" and promises them the kingdom of heaven.

In contrast, the power brokers and establishment bosses, wise in their own eyes, draw sharp, confrontational criticism from Jesus. Actually, he leans harder on self-righteous religious leaders than on anyone else. Their assumed superiority and arrogant lording-it-over "sinners" provoke him to anger and stinging rebuke.

Jesus cherishes the lowly and unlearned, those who accept his message at face value. At one point he prays, "I praise you, Father, Lord of heaven and earth, because you have hidden these things from the wise and learned, and revealed them to little children. Yes, Father, for this is what you were pleased to do" (Matt. 11:25–26). Those who value their importance, self-sufficiency, and self-righteousness tend to close off the good news about God's kingdom. They're sure they don't need it, and don't pick up on it.

The next statement by Jesus, on the surface, seems arbitrarily selective. He says, "All things have been committed to me by my Father. No one knows the Son except the Father, and no one knows the Father except the Son and those to whom the Son chooses to reveal him" (v. 27). That sounds like the Son of God whimsically picks some while ignoring others. It seems unfair until he finishes the explanation: "Come to me, all you who are weary and burdened, and I will give you rest. Take my yoke upon you and learn from me, for I am gentle and humble in heart, and you will find rest for your souls. For my yoke is easy and my burden is light" (vv. 28–30).

Here lies the beauty of the open invitation. God does not pick his favorites for entrance to his kingdom. He calls each of us. Yet God knows it's the individual's heart attitude that sets up the choice. The condition of each person's ego determines whether his or her invitation feels easy or hard, palatable or unpalatable, attractive or unattractive.

A spectrum of response awaits each person. We tend to start on the left of the response line. We bend toward self-absorption and self-enthronement from birth. Life's ups and downs, successes and failures, either break down or reinforce our self-sufficiency. When Jesus invites us to come, the direction we move reveals our response. If we firmly control our situations and run our agendas, we'll act indifferent or defensive toward Jesus.

On the other hand, if we've lived through shattered dreams and crushed hopes, we might open up. Of course, if we harbor unforgiveness, bitterness, anger, and self-pity, we might turn down Jesus's invitation. We might not recognize his deep compassion or readiness to walk alongside and meet our needs. However, I've often watched in amazement and awe as people release bitterness and anger in a willingness to forgive, and suddenly they're ready for Jesus.

Jesus's Invitation: "Come to Me"
Matthew 11:28–30
Spectrum of Human Response

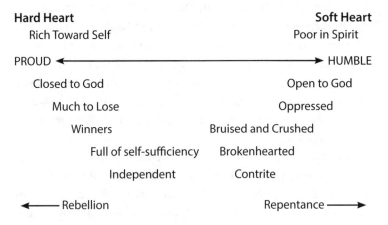

Hard Heart	Soft Heart
Rich Toward Self	Poor in Spirit
PROUD ⟵————————————⟶ HUMBLE	
Closed to God	Open to God
Much to Lose	Oppressed
Winners	Bruised and Crushed
Full of self-sufficiency	Brokenhearted
Independent	Contrite
⟵——— Rebellion	Repentance ———⟶

At first impression, the warmth of God's open arms seems irresistible. Who wouldn't come? Who in their right mind wouldn't take advantage of this offer? And that rips the mask off our problem. Most of us react adversely to this invitation precisely because the ultimate authority invites us. The Bible says he is "the name that is above every name" to which every knee will bow (Phil. 2:9–10). Yet he says, "Come to me, take my yoke upon you and learn from me (Matt. 11:28–29).

Harnessing ourselves to Jesus would obviously mean we are committed to him. We go where he goes and do what he does. Yoked like an ox, a beast of burden? Side by side with Jesus, guess who's going to provide the strength? Absolutely amazing! Here's the chance of a lifetime for the poor in spirit; but a serious challenge for those rich toward self. There's a key concept here. Rest. That's right; "rest for our souls" is what Jesus is offering. That's the opposite of rest-less-ness.

The most popular story Jesus told still hits home.

The biblical Parable of the Prodigal Son, a story we examined in chapter 5 from the older brother's standpoint, best illustrates the open arms waiting behind Jesus's come-to-me invitation. But what about the younger son, the one who wastes his inheritance and desperately needs his father's forgiveness? From that perspective, the story reveals God's heart toward people who go their stubborn way and get lost. Like the prodigal's father, the heavenly Father still loves and waits for his children, even after they reject and desert him.

Because this story plays itself out in every generation, we recognize the youngest son's predicament. It's the heartbreak of rebellion. Loved and protected children, showered with privileges from birth, chronically turn on their parents and demand rights and freedom. This universal pattern among all races, nationalities, and people groups reveals the root problem for us all. Some demonstrate more brash courage than others in acting out rebellion, but all harbor self-focused hearts. Prodigal children illustrate the human race's colossal rebellion against its parent Creator.

God allows freedom of choice.

This demand for an inheritance speaks volumes about the prodigal son. He won't wait until the old man dies to get the money. He wants to spend it while young and fully capable of enjoying it. The interaction also reveals a lot about the father. Under no obligation to grant this outrageous request, the father honors his son's demand. The aging man doesn't attempt to talk the youth out of the money, or leverage a change of mind. He doesn't sever the relationship by disowning his son and kicking him out. He simply hands over the inheritance and releases him.

This acquiescence illustrates how God handles our freedom

of choice, the decision-making ability he trusted us to use wisely. God blesses us with an awesome privilege and responsibility when he fashions us in his image, including self-determination. God dignifies our power and right to choose by not interfering, even when we make painful and destructive choices.

Strong-willed and full of his self-indulgent desires, the prodigal son cashes out and leaves his family far behind. Living in the fast lane, he quickly squanders his money with wine, women, and parties. His lifestyle eventually exacts its toll and leaves him stripped and destitute. Those who call themselves friends discard the young man when his pockets empty out.

Hard times arrive. A famine in the land makes employment opportunities scarce. Finally, in desperation he accepts a job feeding pigs. Imagine the humiliation of a Jewish boy raising pork, and even more disgusting, he drools over the husks and pods tossed to the pigs. He's at rock bottom.

At this point in the story, Jesus says it's the moment the young man "comes to his senses."

The prodigal remembers that his father treats the servants on his estate well. They are not abused. They have shelter and all the food they need. The son mutters to himself, "I made a huge mistake. I need to just go home, back to my father, and tell him the truth: 'Father, I was so wrong. I have sinned against you and God. I am no longer worthy to be called your son. Please, just take me on as one of your hired servants.'" He stands up in the pig squalor, stretches his legs, and heads home.

Still a long way from the house, the young man spots his father running toward him. Filled with compassion, the father throws his arms around the son and kisses him. The son chokes out the little apology speech rehearsed in the hog pen. But his father yells for his servants, "Quick, bring the best robe and put it on him. Put the family ring on his finger. Get some sandals on this man's feet—hurry up! And roast that calf we've been fattening up for the upcoming feast. Let's celebrate! My son is home. He was as good as dead in his selfishness and rebellion, but he is alive again in his repentance. He was lost but now is found." (See Luke 15:11–24; adapted from the NIV.)

Jesus's Teaching on Salvation: *The Rebellious Son*
Luke 15:11–24

Kingdom of Self
- Independent spirit
- Wanted his own way
- Chose to live life as he pleased

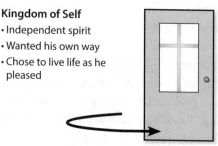

Kingdom of God
Compassionate father ran to his son, embraced him, kissed him, celebrated

- "He came to his senses."
- I will go back
- I will confess
- I will humble myself

THE PRINCIPLE
Grace flows to the humble

At this point it's helpful to notice why and to whom Jesus tells this story. As usual, the critics of Jesus are accusing him of indiscretion as a teacher. Tax collectors and sinners gather to hear him. The Pharisees, Jesus's perpetual detractors, think this marks Jesus as a fraud. So he tells them three stories: the first one about a lost sheep, the second about a lost coin, and the third about a lost son. He ends the first and second stories with this view of God's heart: "I tell you that in the same way there will be more rejoicing in heaven over one sinner who repents than over the ninety-nine righteous persons who do not need to repent" (v. 7). A second time he says, "I tell you, there is rejoicing in the presence of the angels of God over one sinner who repents" (v. 10).

In the third story we're privy to an insider's view of God's feelings about his rebellious children returning home in humble repentance. Once again, when we picture the kingdom realities from the perspective of a wayward son, we view the heart issues and what happens when anybody approaches the waiting heavenly Father.

Pride and humility are revealed in our prayers.

Jesus tells another story about what coming to him is like. His audience comprises people confident of their righteousness and who look down on others. Jesus says, "Two men went up to the temple to pray, one a Pharisee and the other a tax collector. The Pharisee stood up and prayed about himself: 'God, I thank you that I am not like other men—robbers, evildoers, adulterers—or even like this tax collector. I fast twice a week and give a tenth of all I get.' But the tax collector stood at a distance. He would not even look up to heaven, but beat his breast and said, 'God, have mercy on me, a sinner.'"

The Pharisee presents the "I'm unique, I'm an exception, I'm better than others" attitude. Next to this arrogant stereotype stands the humble person God desires. The floodgate of God's gracious love and forgiveness opens through this humble repentance. Without an end to the preoccupation of the self with itself, without a departure from self-in-control pride, God's come-to-me invitation falls on deaf ears. Jesus ends his contrast of the two men with this conclusion: "I tell you that this man [the tax collector], rather than the other, went home justified before God. For all those who exalt themselves will be humbled, and those who humble themselves will be exalted" (Luke 18:10–14).

Jesus's Teaching on Salvation: A Contrast
Luke 18:10–14

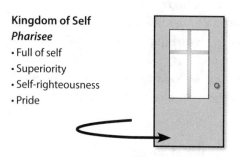

Kingdom of Self
Pharisee
- Full of self
- Superiority
- Self-righteousness
- Pride

Kingdom of God
Tax Collector
- Recognition of his sin
- Confession of sin
- No sign of self-justification
- Humility

The Question
Who is justified before God?

THE PRINCIPLE
"Those who exalt themselves will be humbled, and those who humble themselves will be exalted."

It can't be boiled down more simply than that. God eagerly waits to be reconciled with us. He goes far past halfway in offering a restored relationship. He calls, "Come, come to me. Come home; come back."

God did everything possible to facilitate our return to him. As a just and responsible leader, motivated solely by love, he initiated a plan for our return home. He was "God with us" in Jesus. And when humanity turned on Jesus, he transformed violent rejection into a means of grace. Through his crucifixion he forgave us unilaterally, before anyone recognized or admitted our unfair, abusive behavior toward him. Through his sacrificial death and resurrection, Jesus piled our sin upon himself, suffered justice in our place, and offered pardon and acceptance to anyone who wants to be part of his kingdom.

"Come to me" is God's heart cry. Who will come? Who will return from the "far country" of a self-in-control life?

The brokenhearted, oppressed, disenfranchised, humbled, repentant, and poor in spirit . . . these will come! Whoever brings a contrite heart will find the amazing mercy, love, and joy of a celebrating Father.

Will you come?

EPILOGUE

THE END OF RESTLESSNESS

By this time I hope you're ready to respond to Jesus and choose His magnificent kingdom. You've examined his message and qualities as a leader. Through conversations with individuals he met, you've learned the crucial value of committing your life to him. The next step belongs to you.

The graph below shows the places individuals reside in regard to Jesus. People who become Jesus followers engage in a process leading to a point-in-time decision. They repent—change their mind about allowing God to restore and manage their lives. After this pivotal choice or transaction, a day-to-day journey begins. It is a lifestyle of ongoing surrender to God's leadership.

Where would you place yourself on the following spectrum (see page 184)? Are you ready to move on and take the next step in the process of repentance? You have nothing to lose but your own agenda and its persistent restlessness.

Identifying Your Heart
Bowing and Believing

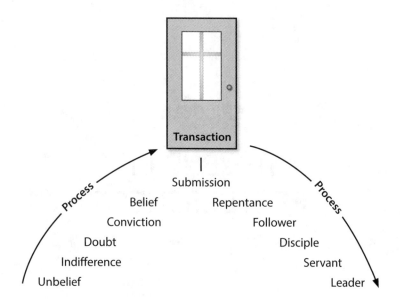

The postponement ploy is deadly.

At this point, watch out for the greatest trick of the chronic self-in-control heart. It tries to dilute or diffuse God's initiatives. When the mind recognizes God's truth, when the conscience fills with conviction, when the emotions feel the tug of unconditional love, small but powerful words zoom into our thoughts. "But what about . . . ?"

- "Yes, God is God, the Creator, Owner, Operator, and Supreme Leader of the universe. But what about . . . ?"
- "Yes, the Bible is God's message. It says a lot of good and important things. But what about . . . ?"

- "Yes, Jesus Christ is who he claimed to be. He is God-in-human-form. He provides salvation to all who will accept his gift of forgiveness, acceptance, and eternal life in his kingdom. But what about . . . ?"
- "Yes, I'm running my life, my way. I've built a world that revolves around me. I know this personal kingdom keeps me at odds with God and I know I am out from under his leadership. But what about . . . ?"

The reluctant or resistant heart dilutes, diffuses, dissipates, distracts, delays, discusses. In essence, a self-in-control heart hits the pause button.

It's a great technique that works. You'll hear this language in the university, the halls of government, the courtroom, the boardroom, and the broadcast studio. "But what about . . . ?" With your eternal destiny at stake, why go there? Why wait longer? Time will eventually run out.

Restlessness can give way to peace. Jesus shows us how this can happen. The choice is yours.

DISCUSSION QUESTIONS

Chapter One: Restless About God

1. Have you ever experienced restlessness or inner anxiety? What do you think contributed to that experience?
2. Does the statement, "Everybody has a kingdom. Everybody!" ring true to you? What were the kingdoms of your father and mother? What do you think yours might be?
3. Would you be more impressed with Jesus if he had come as royalty and lived a life of privilege in a palace? Why have most people down through history accepted the pomp and splendor of human kings and queens?
4. Why is a humble version of God attractive?

Chapter Two: Playing God

1. Would a spirituality that "shuts down evil and empowers good" be inviting to you? Explain.
2. What does our obsession with control do to our marriages and families? What do control issues have to do with national and international politics?

3. Why does doing our own thing and going our own way feel like freedom?
4. What is your definition of sin? If you don't like the word *sin*, what do you think is wrong with human beings?
5. Do you personally long for perfect government and an end to injustice? What do you think it will take to make it happen?

Chapter Three: Walking Away from God

1. I've suggested that the rich young ruler might have been returning from a funeral when he met Jesus. What's your best guess as to why he asked Jesus what he must do to have eternal life?
2. When have you thought seriously about the end of life or the possibility of an afterlife?
3. If you had the chance, would you ask Jesus what you need to do to have eternal life?
4. Do you think Jesus set the bar too high for the rich young man? Why is wealth and the power it brings a huge barrier to receiving God's kingdom?
5. What was Chris, the young politician, afraid would happen if he started following Jesus?
6. One of our most common fears rises from the suspicion that if we give God control of our lives we won't enjoy them. Where does that fear originate?

Chapter Four: Arguing with God

1. Why do you think Jesus provoked the religious experts he encountered? What was behind their constant attempts to discredit him?
2. What inclines intellectuals and experts of various kinds to assume superiority over others?
3. When people are sure they are right, how do they often treat the people they believe are wrong?
4. In the story of the university professor, Alex Thurmond,

we saw a man who was absolutely sure of himself and his worldview. What do you think played the biggest part in his change of heart?

5. The kingdom of the mind is one of the most resistant to God's kingdom. How do you explain the way people with a high IQ seem to find it hard to find faith in God credible? Is it really that a Creator God doesn't make sense or is it that he gets in their way?

Chapter Five: Angry with God

1. Our sense of fair play or justice can take us far from God. Why is God so often blamed for suffering, inequality, and injustice?

2. When Clarissa saw her friend being called to account for her lifestyle choices, Clarissa became extremely angry. Why does accountability anger people?

3. Why do you think God arranged the story of the birth of Jesus so that King Herod's attempt to kill the infant comes right on the heels of the visit of the Wise Men (Matt. 2:1–12)? What is it about our need to protect our personal kingdoms that makes us all dangerous?

4. Kingdoms of bitterness, unforgiveness, and revenge are also very difficult to abandon. Have you harbored a grudge or a thirst for revenge for past hurts that now seems impossible to let go?

5. Why is accepting God's forgiveness tied so closely to our willingness to forgive others?

Chapter Six: Blaming God

1. Have you ever had someone suggest that an illness you've struggled with is "in your head"?

2. What do you think went through the mind of the man lying beside the Pool of Bethesda when Jesus asked him, "Do you want to get well?"

3. Why do you think Jesus connected the man's sickness to his sin? In what ways can sin make us sick?

4. Revisit the story of Carol, the professional street person, what do you think about the observation that victimhood is often about power?

5. Self-pity is a symptom of a type of inner kingdom that is extremely common. How have you avoided feeling sorry for yourself and the accompanying you-owe-me attitude? How would you advise others who might be stuck there?

Chapter Seven: Abusing God

1. Jason has a personal philosophy based on his parents' training and faith. He calls it "getting on the good side of authority." How has complying with the powers-that-be in your life worked for you? How has resisting authorities affected you?

2. Can you identify Jason's kingdom? What makes its grip so powerful?

3. Why is the world of education and science so often intimidating to people of faith?

4. What do we think we gain by "edging God out" (EGO)?

5. What would entering the door to peace in God's kingdom cost you? What would you gain?

Chapter Eight: At Odds with God

1. In the story of the tenants, the landowner represents God, and the servants left in charge of the vineyard represent humans. Jesus is pointing out that this is the way our Creator sees our attempts to take over our lives and his world. Do you think this is an accurate assessment? If you put yourself in God's place as the owner and operator of the universe, does that change the way you see the situation?

2. Saul was so sure he was right he was willing to kill people who differed, an attitude we see behind terrorism today.

Why is it so hard to be completely convinced that you are right and yet not hurt the people you believe are wrong?

3. Sometimes we hear people say, "I just wish God would speak to me in an audible voice." Why does Saul's experience on the road to Damascus lead us to suspect it might not be the best way to hear from God?

4. How do you explain why humanly devised religious kingdoms are so hard to exchange for the real kingdom of God?

5. Does it surprise you that religion proves to be a perfect place to build and hide personal kingdoms? Why or why not?

Chapter Nine: Curious About God

1. Empty religion thrives on appearances and performance. Nicodemus climbed to the top of his religious culture only to realize he was missing something significant. His heart hungered for a genuine relationship with God, not mere religious routines. Have you ever gotten tired of keeping up appearances in some area of your life, maybe even your religious life? Does the fresh-start language of being *born again* sound organic and earthy enough to spark your interest? Why or why not?

2. As far as we know, Jesus never used the "you must be born again" language with anyone else. What was it about Nicodemus that prompted Jesus to use this approach?

3. Why do you think people who gravitate toward religion try to impress God with what they can do? Why is "doing the best you can" so common to all religions?

4. Jesus left Nicodemus with the clear message that he was the only hope of ever entering the kingdom of God. He used the story of the dying Israelites and the brass serpent on a pole as the only antidote to underline this reality. What do you have the hardest time accepting about the idea that Jesus is the only way back to God?

5. In your physical birth your mother did all the work. You benefited from her effort and pain. Jesus is offering to guide you through another kind of birth, a spiritual one. Because of amazing love he provides the effort and the painful sacrifice so you can enter into his kingdom. You receive the benefits of his effort. Have you had what you would call a new birth through repentant faith in what Jesus has done for you? Describe your experience.

Chapter Ten: *Thirsty for God*

1. Maslow famously created the well-known hierarchy of human need. Some have noticed that our needs are often what bring us to God. What needs do you think the woman at the well had?
2. What is an inner thirst about?
3. How did Jesus meet the Samaritan woman's need?
4. What do you think motivated the second woman mentioned in this chapter? When she washed Jesus's feet with her tears and wiped them with her hair, what was she expressing?
5. How big a deal is forgiveness and a second chance to you?
6. Do you see yourself as one who needs to be forgiven much or little by God? How is your answer to that question connected to your love for him?

Chapter Eleven: *Questioning God*

1. I have said, "Skepticism is a position of power." Does this strike you as true or as a defensive criticism? Be honest. When have you used skepticism to postpone a decision or action?
2. The tension in the New Testament is the result of conflict between Jesus and his detractors. It's there on every page. Why was so much hostility aimed at an obviously good man?
3. Why is expressing your doubts a clever way to hide your personal agenda and delay faith?

4. Thomas, the classic doubter, got personal attention from the resurrected Lord. Do you think Jesus cares about your confusion and struggle with doubt?

5. Why does remembering what God has already done for you and those around you help with what is going on right now?

6. Why do you think the positive advances in science made by Christians are treated with loud silence?

7. If a person is more interested in questions than answers, what is really going on in their heart?

Chapter Twelve: Seeing God

1. How is physical blindness a good analogy for spiritual blindness? Where does the analogy fall short?

2. What did the story of the blind beggar in John 9 have to do with physical blindness and what did it say about spiritual blindness?

3. In Jack's story, why did his girlfriend hurt him so badly when she was merely being consistent with his lifestyle philosophy?

4. Why was Harry, Jack's AA sponsor, able to get through to him? What is so powerful about people who have a similar story to our own and who know all the tricks of self-talk?

5. Self-imposed blindness likes to pretend that darkness is really light and light is darkness. It's the classic dodge of changing the price tags, revising history, or redefining reality. Do you want to see the light of God's kingdom with the eyes of your heart? Think deeply about how the ex-blind man *saw* who Jesus was. We see the door to peace with our hearts. We enter it by confessing Jesus is our Lord and Savior. Have you made that choice?

Chapter Thirteen: Ready to Meet God

1. I know Ted Bundy and Jeffrey Dahmer are extreme examples of second-chance grace and forgiveness. Why is it so

hard for us to believe they repented and were forgiven by God?

2. Why is the faith of the thief on the cross beside Jesus hard to accept? Jailhouse professions of faith are considered a joke by many in law enforcement. And yet, many of them are real and produce changed lives.

3. Why are we naturally skeptical of last minute, deathbed conversions?

4. Does Jesus's prayer from the cross, "Father, forgive them," help you understand the kind of leader he is? If Jesus is God and is deliberately revealing what God the Father is like, does this prayer draw you in or push you away?

5. Carl, the convict, is another example of a person who starts far away from God but responds to a message of undeserved love and forgiveness. Do you think you are too far gone to enter the door to peace Jesus says is open to everyone?

Chapter Fourteen: Giving Up to God

1. Zacchaeus is another kind of "rich young ruler." What is so shocking about the announcement he made after having lunch with Jesus?

2. In order for any of us to give up what we already have, we must be convinced that something better is available. Jesus called the kingdom of God a treasure hidden in a field for which a man was willing to sell everything he owned to possess it. He then told of a pearl merchant who found the perfect pearl and sold everything he had in order to purchase it. For what would you give everything in order to possess it?

3. Would you be willing to trade kingdoms with Bill Gates? If so, why not with Jesus, who makes Bill Gates look like a street person?

4. Have you ever prayed an honest faith/surrender prayer like Brent? If so, what did you actually tell God? What happened as a result?

5. Many of us try to keep our kingdoms and add God's to ours. Have you tried that? Why doesn't it work?
6. Zacchaeus "sold the farm" to follow Jesus. He went all in. Are you at that point yet?

Chapter Fifteen: Respect for God

1. The kinds of faith I list at the beginning of this chapter are very common. Which is closest to your faith?
2. The Roman Centurion is clearly operating on a belief that Jesus is not a mere man. Who does he think Jesus is?
3. His grasp of the principle of authority and what it means to be "under authority" is brilliant. Why does Jesus call this grasp of how authority works *great faith*?
4. Marv came to the same conclusion as the centurion. He also treated Jesus as if he was God and it totally changed his life. Why is bowing part of believing? Why is repentance (changing your mind about who ought to be in control) part of real faith?
5. God orchestrated Marv's life in such a way that he had the best possible opportunity to repent and embrace the kingdom. What has God been doing in your life to get your attention?

Chapter Sixteen: Coming to God

1. What attitude of heart attracts the mercy and compassion of Jesus? Why do you think he said, "Blessed are the poor in spirit, for theirs is the kingdom of heaven" (Matt. 5:3)?
2. In the Spectrum of Response graphic on page 175, "rich toward self" is on one side and "poor in spirit" is on the other. I am depicting the kind of heart that draws the attention and compassion of Jesus. Can you locate your heart on this spectrum?
3. Are you surprised that Jesus resists the proud but gives grace to the humble?

4. If you have been a prodigal child, what took you on your journey to the "far country"?
5. What do you think "coming to your senses" has to be about?
6. Why is this particular story one of the most popular and famous tales in history?
7. In the story of the Pharisee and the tax collector, Jesus is teaching us how to enter the door to God's kingdom. His punch line goes like this: "Those who exalt themselves will be humbled, and those who humble themselves will be exalted." We come to God in an attitude of surrender to his role as leader. Have you tried to get in on his forgiveness without giving him permission to lead? It never works, does it? He is God! Let him be God to you in everything all the time.

Epilogue: The End of Restlessness

1. As you look at the progression of heart attitudes in the figure on page 184, on which side of the cross (the transaction) would you place your heart?
2. Can you identify with the process of choices that make up your journey through the door to peace?
3. Jesus opened the way into his kingdom by taking your guilt at the cross. Have you come right up to the door he created and stalled? The "yes . . . but" postponement ploy is exceedingly common and dangerous. Are you stuck right at the entrance to God's kingdom?
4. If you have gotten this far, you are about to finish this book. Please don't close it without entering the kingdom! Read "A Fresh Start with God" (page 197) carefully. It is a practical guide but you must take the initiative on your own. You are face-to-face with life's most important choice . . . repentant faith. Ahead of you is life in the incredible kingdom of God that Jesus talked so much about. Take the next step! Open your hands. Let go of your kingdom so you can receive his.

A FRESH START WITH GOD

So how do you begin a fresh start with God? These steps can guide you:

1. Talk to God about how you've treated him. Apologize for your disrespect, defiance, or indifference. Give him credit for your existence: life, body, mind, emotions, unique abilities, and power of choice. Ask for the forgiveness he offers through Jesus and tell him you accept his leadership.
2. Ask God to make your heart his home. Tell him you want to draw close to him, now and always. Explain that you value the joy of knowing him and his companionship. Be sensitive to what gives him joy or pain in the ways you talk to and treat him. Give him permission to love and lead you.
3. Take his message seriously. God communicates with us through the Bible. Read it, asking him to make its meaning alive for you. Listen for his quiet voice and do what he says.
4. Spend time with people who love and follow Jesus. As you grow in your relationship with God, make friends with people also committed to his leadership. Attend a church

that is a true community of Christ followers. Not all Christian churches live in surrender to God's leadership. Find one that embraces the supreme value of letting Jesus lead in everything.

When you empower God in your life, a process begins. During your life you will encounter many choices to follow God's lead. If you take back control, admit it, turn around, and start over with fresh surrender. This is the joy of repentance. This is the miracle of his love. This is the assurance of eternal life with him.

Welcome, welcome to God's kingdom!

ABOUT THE AUTHOR

Jan David Hettinga served as the lead pastor of Northshore Community Church near Seattle from 1979 to 2008. During his years of ministry at Northshore he led the congregation into a church planting movement. After retirement he continued to lead the Northsound Church Planting Network, which has planted twenty-two churches in the region since 1996 with more on the drawing board. Currently he is the leadership development pastor at Cascade Community Church in Monroe, Washington, one of the daughter churches.

The focus of Jan's teaching is the life-transforming power of the kingdom gospel of Jesus.

In 2005 Jan earned his doctor of ministry degree in Transformational Leadership at Bakke Graduate University in Seattle. He teaches kingdom leadership and church multiplication wherever and whenever God opens the doors.

The dynamic power of the kingdom message was the subject of Jan's first book, *Follow Me: Experience the Loving Leadership of Jesus* (NavPress, 1996). Writing is a life-giving outlet for Jan that flows from a passion to communicate with as many people as possible.

Jan and his wife, Scharme, have three married children and eleven grandchildren. They enjoy spending time with family and friends, reading, walking, and exploring the world with an eye for strategic opportunities for sharing the good news of Christ's kingdom and multiplying churches.